SMARTER BALANCED

GRADE 4

By Jo Ann Robichaud, M.Ed., and Susan Tozier, CAGS, M.Ed.

T0116651

About the Math Author

Jo Ann Robichaud has been an educator for over twenty-eight years. She has taught kindergarten through eighth grade and has worked as an administrator. Currently she teaches a contained fifth-grade class and her area of expertise is elementary math. Jo Ann obtained her Bachelor of Science degree in Elementary Education and her Master's degree in Administration and Supervision from Plymouth State College in New Hampshire. She has been fully immersed in the Common Core Standards and the Smarter Balanced Assessments for the past three years. Robichaud has a passion for assisting students and helping them become successful in their learning. She would like to thank her family, especially her husband Wesley and two daughters, Christine and Michelle, for believing in her and for their love and support while she was writing this book.

About the English Language Arts Author

Susan Tozier is a literacy specialist for pre-Kindergarten through grade five. During her thirty years as an educator, she also taught fourth grade and fourth-fifth multiage. Susan holds a Bachelor of Science in Elementary Education from the University of Maine at Orono, a Master of Education in Reading, and a Certificate of Advanced Graduate Study in Educational Administration and Supervision from the University of New Hampshire. Her experience with students, English Language Arts curriculum development, and school-wide Smarter Balanced Assessments implementation assisted her with authoring this book. Susan lives in New Hampshire, but her heart belongs in Maine! She is grateful for the support of her friends and family during the writing of this book.

The Smarter Balanced Performance Task Scoring Rubrics on pages 108–111, 113–116, and 118–121 are reprinted with permission courtesy of The Regents of the University of California. The publishing of this information does not represent an endorsement of products offered or solicited by Barron's Educational Series, Inc.

© Copyright 2017 by Barron's Educational Series, Inc.

All rights reserved.
No part of this publication may be reproduced or distributed in any form or by any means without the written permission of the copyright owner.

All inquiries should be addressed to:
Barron's Educational Series, Inc.
250 Wireless Boulevard
Hauppauge, NY 11788
www.barronseduc.com

ISBN: 978-1-4380-0922-3

Library of Congress Control Number: 2016945484

Date of Manufacture: October 2016
Manufactured by: B11R11

Printed in the United States of America
9 8 7 6 5 4 3 2 1

10%
POST-CONSUMER
WASTE
Paper contains a minimum
of 10% post-consumer
waste (PCW). Paper used
in this book was derived
from certified, sustainable
forestlands.

Contents

The Purpose and Organization of This Guide

Thank you for purchasing this book! It was written in collaboration by two veteran teachers to support both fourth-grade students and their parents in preparing for the Smarter Balanced assessments (SBA). This assessment is now given in many states and was developed by the Smarter Balanced Assessment Consortium (SBAC), which is a group of states and dedicated educators who collaborated to design this assessment. Chapter 2 of this book offers an overview of the Smarter Balanced assessments and explains why, when, and how it is given. Next, Part One of this book is dedicated to explaining and preparing a fourth-grade student (referred to as "you") for the English Language Arts (ELA) section of this assessment. Then, Part Two of this book is dedicated to the Mathematics section of the assessments. Each part offers explanatory material, sample questions, key vocabulary necessary for a fourth grader to understand, and a sample test that covers both the computer-adaptive and performance task sections of the assessments. Each assessment is followed by a chapter containing detailed answer explanations for every question on the test. Appendices A and B provide full-text versions of the Grade 4 Common Core State Standards for both ELA and Math, as well as the K−12 Standards for Mathematical Practices.

CHAPTER 2

An Introduction to the Smarter Balanced Assessments

What Are the Smarter Balanced Assessments?

The Smarter Balanced assessments are tests that are given toward the end of grades 3−8 and grade 11 that measure student learning and knowledge of English language arts/literacy and mathematics.

Over the past few years, schools across the United States have started implementing new academic standards to ensure that students graduating high school are prepared for college and the workplace. This set of academic standards, known as the Common Core State Standards (CCSS), consists of learning goals that outline what a student should know and be able to do at the end of each grade. The standards are designed to provide a clear path for students to gain the proficiency that is required to learn increasingly complex material in English Language Arts (ELA) and Mathematics at each grade level. The CCSS challenge students to develop a deeper understanding of various subject matter, learn how to think critically, and apply what they have learned to the real world.

To help students, parents, and teachers recognize whether students are on the path to success with the academic standards at each grade level, states joined together as groups to develop tests that measure student achievement. One of these groups is called the *Smarter Balanced Assessment Consortium*, which is often abbreviated as the "SBAC." The actual assessments are more commonly referred to as "Smarter Balanced assessments" or "Smarter Balanced."

> For more information about the Smarter Balanced Assessment Consortium, go to *www.smarterbalanced.org*.

The Smarter Balanced Assessment Consortium, with input from K−12 teachers, higher education faculty, and other experts, developed next-generation assessments to accurately measure student progress toward college and career readiness in English Language Arts and Mathematics. Next-generation assessments are online assessments that include technology-enhanced, interactive assessment items. The Smarter Balanced assessments are aligned to the Common Core State Standards. The results of the Smarter Balanced assessments help educators, parents, and students gather information about students' strengths and struggles in literacy and math. The information is used to continuously improve teaching and learning and to help ensure that students are prepared when they graduate from high school. The Smarter Balanced assessment system was fully implemented in the spring of 2015.

For more information about the Common Core Standards, go to www.corestandards.org.

How and When Are the Smarter Balanced Assessments Given?

All Smarter Balanced assessments (except for the classroom activities that introduce the Performance Tasks) are administered using computers. Depending on your school, you might complete testing in your school's computer lab or in your classroom where you and your classmates each will use a device (such as a laptop, tablet, or Chromebook).

The Smarter Balanced assessments consist of two parts for each subject: a **Computer-Adaptive Test** and a **Performance Task**.

The **Computer-Adaptive Test (CAT)** is taken online and customizes a set of test questions just for you! There will be questions in a variety of formats that will be adapted, or adjusted, for you based on your answers to previous questions. The question formats for the CAT may require multiple-choice answers, constructed-response tasks (which are short written answers), or technology-enhanced responses, which require you to select answers by clicking and highlighting a specific section or dragging and dropping the correct answer to a certain spot.

The **Performance Task (PT)** is a collection of questions and activities that are connected to a single topic or scenario. These questions and activities will allow you to combine your critical-thinking and problem-solving skills. The Performance Task begins with a classroom activity with your teacher and classmates. The classroom activity is a discussion that provides you with an introduction to the Performance Task topic and helps prepare you for the next part of the assessment by providing background information and key vocabulary. After the classroom activity for ELA, you will complete research online by reading about a real-world situation. Then, you will apply your knowledge and skills and use evidence from what you read to answer two to three questions and respond to a writing prompt. After the Math classroom activity, you will answer multistep questions and perform activities with many parts that deal with that specific theme or scenario. The Performance Task part of the Smarter Balanced assessments is not Computer-Adaptive.

> To see examples of performance tasks, go to
> www.smarterbalanced.org/sample-items-and-performance-tasks.

The Smarter Balanced assessments are administered during the last 12 weeks of the school year. The Smarter Balanced assessments are not timed, but it is estimated that, for students in grades 3−5, the English Language Arts assessment will take a total of 4 hours, and the Math assessment will take a total of 3 hours. In addition, there will be a brief classroom activity to introduce the topic of the Performance Task for each Language Arts and Math. Testing is broken up into multiple testing sessions on multiple days. Testing occurs in multiple sessions, so you will typically spend 1−2 hours per day on the assessments over a few days. Every school may approach the scheduling differently.

Table 2-1 below shows the expected testing times for students in grades 3−5.

Table 2-1. Expected Testing Times for Students in Grades 3-5

	Computer-Adaptive Test		Classroom Activity	Performance Task		Total
	Session 1	Session 2		Session 3	Session 4	
ELA	1 hour	1 hour	30 min	1 hour	1 hour	4 hours
Math	1 hour	1 hour	30 min	1 hour		3 hours

It is important to remember that these are estimates of test lengths. Remember: The tests are not timed. You have as much time as you need to complete the tests.

How Can You Prepare?

You can prepare by reading this guide and answering the sample questions, so you understand what you are expected to know. Along with using this guide, one of the biggest things you can do is increase your technology skills. You can do this by practicing similar online assessments or activities where you interact with technological elements to answer questions. For example, find the types of questions or activities where you need to click your selection, drag and drop items, or select points on a number line or graph. Table 2-2 contains a list of suggested online resources to help you practice.

Table 2-2. Online Resources to Help You Practice for the Smarter Balanced Assessments

Skills	Internet Links
Keyboarding and Mouse Skills	www.learningfarm.com www.funbrain.com www.bealearninghero.org/skill-builder www.abcya.com www.mathisfun.com www.helpingwithmath.com
Test Practice and Skill Building	www.IXL.com www.ThatQuiz.org www.khanacademy.org www.smarterbalanced.org/practice-test www.arcademics.com www.learningfarm.com

You should listen to and learn from your teachers all the time. They have carefully prepared your lessons and are there to guide and support you in the development of your skills. They know where you are succeeding and where you need help, so follow their expert guidance and don't be afraid to ask for help!

How Can Parents Help Prepare and Support Their Child?

Below are some tips for parents to help prepare and support your child:

- Help your child develop good homework and study habits.
- Provide a quiet, comfortable spot to study at home.
- Read with your child and have your child read to you a variety of materials, including both fiction and informational texts.
- Provide opportunities for your child to use a PC, laptop, Chromebook, iPad, etc. The Smarter Balanced assessment is given online, so your child needs to be comfortable with whatever testing device his or her school will be using during the assessment process. Your child should be familiar with typing skills and using the mouse, touchpad, and/or touchscreen to select items, drag and drop items, highlight, scroll, and draw.
- Monitor your child's progress in school, and, if she needs extra support on particular skills, look for tutoring opportunities, after school help, or other resources.
- Ask your child's teacher for activities to do at home that will help prepare your child for this assessment.
- View samples of Smarter Balanced test questions and acquire information about the format of the assessments at *www.smarterbalanced.org*
- Discuss with your child the importance of this test, but assure him that there is no reason to be afraid or anxious. Tell him that you have great expectations for him and that you are there to support him.
- Make sure that your child gets plenty of sleep and eats a well-balanced breakfast before each of the test sessions.
- When you receive the test results, review the scores with your child. Take the time to discuss areas of strength and areas where there is room for improvement. Include the teacher in the discussion when needed. Understand that test scores are only one "snapshot" of what a child is capable of on a given day. Scores can be affected by the way your child was feeling during the test session or in a particular test setting. Assessments are useful, but they should not be the only factor in determining academic progress.

What If My Child Has Special Needs?

Do not worry. The SBAC has written these assessments with proper accommodations built in for students with disabilities and with English language learners in mind. In fact, it contains the most complete collection of accessibility and accommodations resources ever included in a K−12 assessment to date. This assessment was designed to meet students' needs noted by the Individualized Education Program (IEP), acknowledged by school personnel, or written in a 504 plan. For more information on this, visit *www.smarterbalanced.org/parents-students/support-for-under-represented-students*.

IMPORTANT NOTE

In this book, we have tried to give you the most up-to-date information on the fourth-grade Smarter Balanced assessments. However, this information is subject to change at any time during or after the publication of this book. Please bookmark the following websites to use as primary resources in your test preparation:

www.smarterbalanced.org

www.corestandards.org

PART ONE
English Language Arts

What Every Fourth Grader Needs to Know About English Language Arts

CHAPTER 3

Overview

This chapter will provide you with a summary of what you need to understand and be able to do to be successful on the English Language Arts section of the Smarter Balanced assessments. It includes information about phonics and word recognition, fluency, text types, writing, and research.

You have already learned a lot in kindergarten, first grade, second grade, and third grade! During fourth grade, you will continue to develop your skills as a reader, writer, and researcher.

In fourth grade, you will improve how you figure out words and how to read more quickly and accurately. You will read more challenging fiction and nonfiction texts. You will analyze the books and articles that you read. *Analyzing the text* means that you think about the messages an author tells you in the text and how it relates to other things you already know. You will compare texts to each other and make connections between the texts. You will work to clearly communicate your thoughts when writing. You will write about more than just facts; you will also provide details, make connections, and express your ideas and opinions to strengthen your writing. As a researcher, you will investigate information about different topics. You will take notes and organize the information you learn about a topic. Then, you will write about the information you learned.

Your teacher will always be there to guide and support you, but, as a fourth grader, you will be encouraged to be more independent in your learning. Fourth grade is an exciting year where you will learn a great deal!

The following sections are the fourth-grade expectations you will need to understand and be able to demonstrate in different areas of reading and writing.

Phonics and Word Recognition

Expectations

- [ ] Use word-decoding strategies to read unfamiliar words.

- [ ] Recognize that letters and combinations of letters make different sounds.

- [ ] Use your knowledge of consonant blends, long-vowel patterns, and short-vowel patterns to decode words.

- [ ] Analyze the structure of words by finding compound words, base words, prefixes, suffixes, and syllables.

- [ ] Use your analysis of word structure to help you decode unfamiliar, multisyllabic words.

Terms to Know

- **Phonics:** the study of the relationship between letters and the sounds they represent.
- **Word recognition:** the ability to recognize written words correctly and effortlessly.
- **Consonant blend:** a group of two or three consonants in words that each keep their own consonant sound, but their sounds are read together quickly. Consonant blends include *bl, br, ch, ck, cl, cr, dr, fl, fr, gh, gl, gr, ng, nth, ph, pl, pr, sc, sch, scr, sh, shr, sk, sl, sm, sn, sp, spl, spr, st, str, sw, th, thr, tr, tw, wh,* and *wr.*
- **Long-vowel pattern:** a vowel that sounds like its name. There are many combinations and patterns of letters that can be used to represent long-vowel sounds. Table 3-1 outlines all the ways the long-vowel sounds can be spelled.

Table 3-1. Long-Vowel Sounds

Long a		Long e		Long i		Long o		Long u	
Vowel pattern	Sample word	Vowel pattern	Sample word	Vowel pattern	Sample word	Vowel pattern	Sample word	Vowel pattern	Sample word
a	acorn	e	He	i	hi	o	no	u	duty
a_e	take	e_e	Pete	i_e	bite	o_e	hole	u_e	rule
ai	raid	ea	beach	ie	tie	oa	goat	ew	dew
aigh	straight	ee	meet	igh	high	oe	hoe	eu	feud
ay	say	ei	either	uy	guy	ough	dough	oo	toot
ea	break	ey	key	ui	guide	ow	tow	ou	you
ei	rein	ie	chief	y	why	eau	chateau	ough	through
eig	reign	y	badly	ye	eye	ou	soul	ue	blue
eigh	eight	eo	people	isl-	island			ui	fruit
ey	they	i	ski	ai	aisle			uu	vacuum
e	café			ay	aye aye			wo	two
				ei	feisty				

- **Short-vowel pattern:** a vowel that does not say its letter name. Short-vowel sounds match the letters a, e, i, o, and u when there is no silent e at the end of a word or when the vowel is alone between consonants. Short vowels are almost always represented by just a single vowel, but there are a few exceptions. Table 3-2 will help you recognize the short-vowel sounds.

Table 3-2. Short-Vowel Sounds

Short a		Short e		Short i		Short o		Short u	
Vowel pattern	Sample word	Vowel pattern	Sample word	Vowel pattern	Sample word	Vowel pattern	Sample word	Vowel pattern	Sample word
a	jam	e	let	i	sit	o	not	u	sun
a	plan	e	them	i	think	o	clock	u	trunk
a	glass	e	stretch	i	fizz	o	doll	u	bunch
a _ _ e	badge	ea	bread			o _ _ e	dodge	o	front
						a	calm	ou	touch
								oo	flood
								o _ e	love

- **Compound word:** a combination of two or more words that function as a single unit of meaning, such as "waterspout" or "loudspeaker."
- **Structure of words:** how words are formed, including prefixes, suffixes, and other meaningful parts. Many words in the English language have been borrowed from other languages. The origins are usually Latin or Greek. A word can have three parts: a base word, a prefix, and a suffix.

  o **Base word:** a word in its simplest form. It has nothing added to it. Some people call base words *root words*. Examples of base words include "happy," "view," and "write."

  o **Prefix:** a word part that is added to the *front* of a base word. Adding a prefix to a base word makes a new word and changes the meaning of the base word. Examples of prefixes added to base words include *un* + happy = *un*happy, *re* + write = *re*write, and *non* + sense = *non*sense.

  o **Suffix:** a word part that is added to the *end* of a base word. Adding a suffix to a base word makes a new word and changes the meaning of the base word. Examples of suffixes added to base words include pain + *ful* = pain*ful*, care + *less* = care*less*, and friend + *ly* = friend*ly*.

- **Syllable:** a segment of a word that contains only one vowel sound. Each segment of a word is like a "beat" in a word. A word can be made up of only one "beat," or syllable, or many beats. One way to figure out how many beats are in a word is by saying the word slowly and clapping for each beat you hear. Recognizing syllables in words makes the words easier to read and spell. Table 3-3 provides examples of 1-syllable, 2-syllable, 3-syllable, 4-syllable, and 5-syllable words.

Table 3-3. Syllables

1-syllable word examples	dog cheese cake
2-syllable word examples	ho-tel eat-ing sail-boat
3-syllable word examples	beau-ti-ful po-e-try e-lev-en
4-syllable word examples	an-y-bod-y Feb-ru-ar-y mis-un-der-stand
5-syllable word examples	con-grat-u-la-tions re-frig-er-a-tor Ty-ran-o-saur-us

- **Multisyllabic word:** a word that has more than one syllable, such as *ba-nan-a* or hel-i-cop-ter.
- **Decode:** the ability to apply your knowledge of letter-sound relationships, including knowledge of letter patterns, to correctly pronounce written words.
- **Analyze:** to examine a word or text carefully to look for patterns or relationships.

Fluency

Expectations

- [ ] Read with sufficient accuracy and fluency to support comprehension.
- [ ] Read with purpose and understanding.
- [ ] Read prose and poetry aloud with accuracy, rate, and expression.
- [ ] Recognize when a word that you have read previously does not make sense within the text and reread with corrections.
- [ ] Use context clues to know if you are reading accurately and can self-correct when necessary.

Terms to Know

- **Fluency:** the ability to read text accurately, quickly, and with proper expression. When you are a fluent reader, your brain can put more effort into understanding what you read. Fluency includes:
  - o **Accuracy:** reading a word in a text with no errors.
  - o **Rate:** the speed at which you read.
  - o **Expression:** when you change your voice to show feeling when reading.
- **Comprehension:** understanding what you are reading. This is the ultimate goal for all reading!
- **Prose:** everyday writing that is not poetry. Prose includes sentences and paragraphs.
- **Context clue:** using the words or sentences around an unfamiliar word to help understand the meaning of the word.
- **Self-correct:** when, on your own, you fix a mistake you make when reading.

Types of Texts

The next section will discuss what you need to understand and be able to do with different types of texts. Remember, understanding what you read is the ultimate goal of reading. You need to be aware of whether or not you are understanding what you are reading. Many times, you will have to reread a text to find more information and make your understanding clear. You need to "think about thinking" and know what you clearly understand and what is confusing. You have to go back to the text and reread to help fix information that you do not clearly understand.

No matter what type of text you are reading, an effective reading strategy is to ask yourself questions as you read. Table 3-4 presents some questions to ask yourself before, during, and after reading to help you better understand what you are reading.

Table 3-4. Questions to Ask Yourself Before, During, and After Reading

Before Reading	During Reading	After Reading
Why am I reading this? What is my goal for reading?	How do I feel about the main character?	How did my feelings about the character change?
What do I already know about this type of reading or topic?	Why does a character act or feel a certain way?	How are the character's actions or feelings different than at the beginning of the story?
What clues are in the title and the pictures/illustrations?	What do I think will happen next in the story?	How did the story or information make me feel?
Is this a made-up story or factual information? How do I know?	If this story were a movie, what would it be like?	What is the main part of the story or text?
What will the problem in the story be?	Does the text make sense?	What was the most interesting fact I learned?
What do I think I will learn?	Does the text remind me of anything in my own life?	What message did the author want me to take away from this reading?
	What am I learning that I already knew? What things are new?	
	Why is the author including this information?	

Literature

You will read and understand literature, including stories and poetry, written at the fourth-grade level.

Expectations

- ☐ Read closely and find answers that are "right there" in a text.
- ☐ Read closely and find answers that require an inference.
- ☐ Use details and examples in a text when explaining exactly what the text says or when making an inference from the text.
- ☐ Determine the theme of a story or poem using details in the text.
- ☐ Write a summary using details from the text (without telling every detail).
- ☐ Describe a character, setting, or event in a story in depth by telling specific details in the text (such as a character's thoughts, words, or actions).
- ☐ Make meaning of words and phrases, when reading about characters in a myth, by using clues found within the story.
- ☐ Recognize that poems, drama, and prose use different structural elements and explain their differences.
- ☐ Explain the difference between first- and third-person points of view.
- ☐ Compare and contrast the point of view from which different stories are narrated.
- ☐ Compare and contrast a written text of a story to a video or audio of the text.
- ☐ Compare and contrast stories and myths from different cultures.
- ☐ Compare and contrast similar themes and topics (such as good versus evil) and patterns of events in stories, myths, and traditional literature from different cultures.

Terms to Know

- **Read closely:** when a reader reads a passage very carefully with lots of thinking while reading.
- **Passage:** a paragraph or multiple paragraphs.
- **Inference:** when you make a decision based on specific evidence—details you read, heard in an audio, or viewed in a video that are not directly said. The answer to an inference question is not "right there" in a text, audio, or video. You must do some smart thinking to make an inference. First, you find clues in a text, audio, or video. Then, you add those clues to what you already know about the topic of the question. Next, you make your best decision about what the text, audio, or video is implying (suggesting). You need to be able to support your inference with details from the text, audio, or video.

Here is an example of an inference item:

Kay is pouring flour, eggs, sugar, and butter into a large bowl. She then mixes it with a large wooden spoon. She prepares the batter to be placed in the oven. Make an inference about where Kay is.

- O A.   in the living room
- O B.   in the bedroom
- O C.   in the kitchen
- O D.   in the garage

The passage gives you clues: "flour," "eggs," "sugar," "butter," "bowl," "mixes," "batter," and "oven." There is a good chance that you already know that these clues are about making a cake. You also probably know that cakes are made in a kitchen. So, by thinking about the clues and what you already know, you would make the inference that Kay is *in the kitchen*, choice C.

Understanding how to make an inference is a really important skill to know to be successful on the Smarter Balanced assessments!

- **Details:** specific information you read in a text, hear on a video, or see on a video.
- **Theme:** the main message or idea of a story that teaches you about life and the world through the characters and the events in the story.
- **Summary:** a short retelling of the main ideas or events in a passage. When you write a summary, use your own words, not the author's. A good summary tells only the important details from the passage and tells the events in the correct order.
- **Character:** the people or animals in a passage. The text tells a reader how a character acts, thinks, or feels. Characters help move a story along.
- **Setting:** the time and place in which events in a passage happen.
- **Event:** something that has happened or is going to happen in a passage. When an author puts events in order to make a story, he or she has created a *plot*. The different parts of a plot are:
  - **Rising action:** the events that happen at the beginning of a story.
  - **Conflict/problem:** the problem that is faced by a character or characters.
  - **Climax/turning point:** the part in the plot in which the events get the most exciting.
  - **Resolution:** the final part of the plot in which the problem is solved.

- **Myth:** a made-up story that explains how something came to be in nature, such as where thunder comes from or why snow falls from the sky. Myths often include gods and goddesses and other supernatural characters who have the power to make extraordinary things happen.
- **Prose:** everyday writing that is not poetry. Prose includes sentences and paragraphs.
- **Structural elements:** how certain types of literature are developed and put together.

  The following terms are types of literature and their structural elements:

  - **Narrative:** a story about made-up or real events that happen to a character or characters. Usually, a narrative only shows a part of a character's life.

    These are the elements or parts of a narrative:

    - a beginning, middle, and an end.
    - a problem or a conflict that the character has to solve.
    - a climax or a turning point in which the problem builds up.
    - characters that speak through dialogue or who are described by the narrator.

- sentences and paragraphs instead of stanzas.
- the time and place in which the events happen (setting).
- the main idea or message of the story (theme).

o **Drama** (or a play): a passage that tells a story using the lines characters say to each other, as in a script.

These are the elements or parts of a drama:

- **Cast of characters:** a list near the beginning of the play that shows the characters who appear in the play.
- **Stage setting:** the description of the time and place of the play and what the characters are doing as the scene begins.
- **Dialogue:** the lines that the characters say to each other to move the plot along.
- **Stage directions:** the words that appear in parentheses throughout the play and tell the characters how to act.
- **Scene/act:** a small part of a play in which all actions happen in one place and at one time.

o **Poem:** a passage that often uses rhyme and rhythm.

These are the elements or parts of a poem:

- **Verses:** lines that make up a poem.
- **Stanzas:** a group of lines.
- **Rhyme:** using words that end in the same sound.
- **Rhythm:** the way sound is repeated in a pattern.
- **Meter:** the beat of the poem made by repeating a pattern of syllables.

- **Point of view:** the way the author shows who is telling a story, or whose thoughts and feelings are shown. Some stories are told in first-person point of view, and some are told in third-person point of view.

  o **First-person point of view:** when a character in the story tells the reader the story from his/her point of view. Stories told in first-person point of view use words like "I," "we," and "us."
  o **Third-person point of view:** when a narrator who is not a character tells the reader the story. Stories told in third-person point of view use words like "he," "she," and "they."

- **Compare and contrast:** when you notice what is the same (compare) and what is different (contrast) between different events or passages. Passages can be compared and contrasted by the theme, topic, or events.

Informational Text

You will read and understand informational text, including nonfiction books, magazine/newspaper articles, factual sources, or websites related to history, science, and technology, written at the fourth-grade level.

Expectations

- [ ] Read closely and find answers that are "right there" in a text.

- [ ] Read closely and find answers that require an inference.

- [ ] Use details and examples in a text when explaining exactly what the text means or when making an inference from the text.

- [ ] Analyze an author's words and find details and examples to support both explicit and inferential questions.

- [ ] Determine the main idea of what you read and explain it using details from the text.

- [ ] Write a summary stating the key points of a text.

- [ ] Use specific events and ideas from an informational text to explain what happened and why.

- [ ] Locate and use resources to assist in determining the meaning of general academic words and phrases.

- [ ] Explain events, procedures, ideas, or concepts in a historical, scientific, or technical text, including what happened and why, based on specific information in the text.

- [ ] Describe the overall structure—chronology, comparison, cause/effect, problem/solution—in informational texts.

- [ ] Compare and contrast a firsthand account and a secondhand account of the same historical event or topic and describe the differences in the information provided.

- [ ] Recognize that authors use various formats when presenting information.

- [ ] Interpret the nonfiction features—charts, graphs, diagrams, time lines, animations, or interactive elements on webpages—and explain how the information helps to understand the text.

☐   Explain how the author uses reasons and evidence to support the particular points in a text.

☐   Integrate information from two texts on the same topic to knowledgeably write or speak about the subject.

Terms to Know

- **Read closely:** when a reader reads a passage very carefully with lots of thinking while reading.
- **Passage:** a paragraph or multiple paragraphs.
- **Inference:** when you make a decision based on specific evidence—details you read, heard in an audio, or viewed in a video that are not directly said. The answer to an inference question is not "right there" in a text, audio, or video. You must do some smart thinking to make an inference. First, you find clues in a text, audio, or video. Then, you add those clues to what you already know about the topic of the question. Next, you make your best decision about what the text, audio, or video is implying (suggesting). You need to be able to support your decision or inference with details from the text, audio, or video.
- **Explicit questions:** questions where the answer is easy to find in the passage. These types of questions are often called "right there" questions because you can find the answer stated right there in the text. They often begin with the words "who," "what," "where," or "when."
- **Inferential questions:** questions where the text does not actually tell you the answer, but you can work out the answer by considering the hints and clues in the text in connection with your own knowledge and experience.
- **Main idea:** what the text is mostly about or what the overall message the author is trying to tell you. You may be asked to tell the main idea of a whole passage or tell the main idea of a specific paragraph.
- **Key details:** information that is included to support the main idea by filling in background information or expanding on the topic. Key details can also be called supporting details.
- **Summary:** a short retelling of the main ideas or events in a passage. When you write a summary, use your own words, not the author's. A good summary lists only the important events from a passage and tells the events in the correct order.

- **Event:** something that has happened, or is going to happen, in a passage.
- **Academic words and phrases:** specific words about a topic that will help you understand the topic better. When you read an informational text, look for words that you know are important to the topic. Sometimes these words are in bold. If academic words or phrases are unfamiliar to you, use context clues or a dictionary or glossary to help you figure out what the word means.
- **Procedure:** a step-by-step guide.
- **Concept:** an idea that is explained in a passage.
- **Text structure:** the certain ways an author organizes a passage to help the reader better understand the text.

  Here are four types of text structure that an author may use in a passage:

  1. **Chronological order:** when a passage is written in the order of when the events happened or will happen.
  2. **Compare and contrast:** when a passage is written to show how events, ideas, people, or things are alike or different.
  3. **Cause and effect:** when a passage shows how one thing (the cause) created or led to another thing (the effect).
  4. **Problem and solution:** when a passage shows a problem and tells the reader how to fix it.

- **Compare and contrast accounts:** when different authors write about the same information, idea, or event differently. An *account* is the description of the information, idea, or event. There are two types of accounts:

  o **Firsthand account:** the person writing a text is a part of the events. The passage is written using words like "I" and "we." The author may include his or her feelings and thoughts on the subject.
  o **Secondhand account:** the person writing a text is not a part of the events. The events that the author describes have happened to someone else. The author mostly includes information and facts on the subject.

- **Interpreting information:** An author sometimes includes illustrations to help the reader better understand the text. An illustration may help the reader *interpret the information* in the text. Some illustrations that an author might use include:
    - o **Diagram:** an illustration that identifies the parts of something or shows how something works.
    - o **Chart:** an illustration that shows information in bars, pie charts, or line graphs.
    - o **Time line:** an illustration that shows a list of events and the order in which they happened.

- **Author's reasons and evidence:** parts of a passage where the author gives the readers information about why they should believe what the passage says.
- **Integrate:** combine or mix together.

Writing

In fourth grade, you will write for a range of tasks, purposes, and audiences. You will often write over longer periods of time to give you time for research, reflection, and revision. You will also write for shorter time periods, like a single sitting or a day or two.

You will mainly be doing three types of writing: opinion writing, informational/ explanatory writing, and narrative writing.

Opinion Writing

You will write opinion pieces on topics or texts and support your point of view with reasons and information.

Expectations

- ☐ Determine your opinion or point of view on a topic or text.
- ☐ Include your opinion clearly in the introduction of the topic.
- ☐ Organize your ideas.
- ☐ Support your opinion with facts and details.
- ☐ Connect your opinion and reasons using linking words and phrases.
- ☐ Write a concluding statement or paragraph to support your opinion.

Terms to Know

- **Opinion:** a belief, judgment, or way of thinking about something.

- **Organizational structure for opinion writing:** one way to organize your opinion writing is to use the OREO method:

O = Opinion	
Introduction—a sentence or paragraph in the beginning of your opinion writing. It tells about the topic and your opinion.	
R = Reasons	E = Examples
Reason 1—a sentence stating a reason for your opinion	**Example 1**—an example to support Reason 1
Reason 2—a sentence stating a reason for your opinion	**Example 2**—an example to support Reason 2
Reason 3—a sentence stating a reason for your opinion	**Example 3**—an example to support Reason 3
O = Opinion Again	
Conclusion—a sentence or paragraph that is the final part of a text. It tells the topic and your opinion again. It ties together the beginning of your writing to the end.	

- **Linking words and phrases:** words that connect your reasons and examples. Using linking words helps readers follow your ideas better. Table 3-5 introduces some examples of linking words or phrases that you could use in your opinion writing to connect your reasons and examples.

Table 3-5. Linking Words and Phrases for Opinion Writing

Linking Words When Providing Reasons	
• First	• Another reason
• To start	• Lastly
• To begin with	• Finally
• Second	• One last reason
• Next	• Most importantly
Linking Words When Providing Examples	
• For example	• Additionally
• For instance	• In other words
• In particular	• In fact
• Specifically	• An example is

Information Writing

You will write information pieces to examine a topic and convey ideas and information clearly.

Expectations

☐ Clearly introduce a topic.

☐ Organize related information in paragraphs and sections, including formatting (such as headings), illustrations, and multimedia when useful, to help your reader understand.

☐ Develop the topic with facts, definitions, concrete details, quotations, or other information and examples related to the topic.

☐ Include informational text features and multimedia to help your reader better understand your message.

☐ Link ideas using words and phrases (such as "another," "for example," "also," and "because").

☐ Use topic-specific language and vocabulary to better inform your reader.

☐ Write a concluding statement or paragraph to support your topic.

Terms to Know

- **Organizational structure for information writing:** One way to organize your opinion writing is to use the following method outlined in Table 3-6.

Table 3-6. Organizational Structure for Information Writing

Introduction: a sentence or paragraph in the beginning of your informational writing. It clearly tells the topic.
Fact 1: a paragraph with definitions, concrete details, quotations, or other information and examples related to the topic.
Fact 2: a paragraph with definitions, concrete details, quotations, or other information and examples related to the topic.
Fact 3: a paragraph with definitions, concrete details, quotations, or other information and examples related to the topic.
Conclusion: a sentence or paragraph that is the final part of a written response. It clearly tells about the topic again. It ties together the beginning of your writing to the end of your writing.

- **Formatting:** the use of headings and subheadings to organize informational writing. Headings and subheadings indicate what a section of writing will be about.
- **Multimedia:** a way of expressing an idea using text, audio, and video.
- **Concrete details:** facts, data, or specific information that describes or explains something.
- **Develop the topic with examples:** the use of evidence from a text to support your thinking in informational writing. When you use evidence from a text, it is called "citing" the text. Sentence starters for citing a text in your writing include:

  o The author says . . .
  o The author wrote . . .
  o Based on what I read . . .
  o The illustration shows . . .
  o On page 00, the author said . . .
  o In paragraph 00, the author wrote . . .

Most of the time when writing, you should use your own words to describe information that you learned from an author. If you use the exact words that an author wrote in his or her writing, you must use **quotation marks** around those words in your writing. This help your readers know that you are repeating the author's words and they are not your own. You must also explain where you got the words from the author's text. An example might look like this: *Dogs have an amazing sense of smell. In paragraph 2, the author said "A dog's sense of smell is about 1,000 to 10,000,000 times more sensitive than a human's."*

- **Linking words and phrases:** words that connect your reasons and examples. Using linking words help readers follow your ideas better. Table 3-7 introduces some examples of linking words or phrases that you could use in your information writing to discuss a topic:

Table 3-7. Linking Words and Phrases
for Informational Writing

To Clarify	
• After all	• Specifically
• Clearly	• Usually
• Generally	
To Show a Relationship	
• In comparison	• Likewise
• In the same way	• Similarly
To Link	
• Also	• In addition
• And	• Next
• As an example	• But also
• For example	• So

- **Topic-specific language and vocabulary:** words that are special to your topic.

Narrative Writing

You will write narrative pieces to develop real or imagined experiences or events using effective technique, descriptive details, and clear event sequences.

Expectations

- ☐ Introduce the reader to the topic by clearly identifying the characters, setting, plot, narrator, sensory details, and sequence of events.
- ☐ Orient (set the scene for) the reader by introducing the narrator, characters, and the event/situation that starts the story in motion.
- ☐ Describe experiences and events through character dialogue, helping the reader to better understand.
- ☐ Use a variety of transitional words and phrases to organize the sequence of events.
- ☐ Use specific words or phrases and sensory details to describe experiences and events.
- ☐ Write a logical conclusion.

Terms to Know

- **Narrative:** a story about made-up or real events that happen to a character or characters. Usually, a narrative only shows a part of a character's life.
- **Character:** the people or animals in a passage. The text tells a reader how a character acts, thinks, or feels. Characters help move a story along.
- **Setting:** the time and place in which events in a passage happen.
- **Plot:** events in a narrative. The different parts of a plot are
    - o **Rising action:** the events that happen at the beginning of a story.
    - o **Conflict/problem:** the problem that is faced by a character or characters.
    - o **Climax/turning point:** the part in the plot in which the events get the most exciting.
    - o **Resolution:** the final part of the plot in which the problem is solved.
- **Narrator:** the person who is telling the story in a narrative.
- **Sensory details:** details that include sight, sound, touch, smell, and taste. Writers use the five senses to engage a reader's interest.

- **Sequence of events:** the order in which events happen in a narrative.
- **Dialogue:** the conversation that takes place between characters in a story. Simplified rules about using dialogue include:

  o using quotation marks around the words that the character is saying.
  o using quotation marks to identify who is speaking.
  o indenting for a new paragraph each time the speaker changes.

- **Transition words and phrases:** linking words that connect your ideas together to create a smooth flow in your writing to make it logical and easy to follow. Table 3-8 includes some examples of linking words or phrases you could use in your narrative writing to discuss a topic.

Table 3-8. Transition Words and Phrases
for Narrative Writing

To Show a Relationship	
• In comparison	• Likewise
• In the same way	• Similarly
To Show a Sequence	
• Afterward	• Later
• At first	• Meanwhile
• At the same time	• Next
• Earlier	• Soon
• Finally	• Then
• First of all	• While
To Build Suspense	
• All of a sudden	• Out of the blue
• Before I knew it	• Suddenly
• Just then	• Unexpectedly
• In a flash	• Without warning

- **Conclusion:** an ending to a narrative that ties up the plot.

Producing Writing

No matter what type of writing you do, it should be clear, well-developed, and organized.

Expectations

☐   Identify the writing style that best fits your task, purpose, and audience.

☐   Use organizational structures or graphic organizers to develop writing ideas.

☐   Compose a clear and logical piece of writing that demonstrates your understanding of a specific writing style.

Terms to Know

- **Writing style:** the way a writer writes; the way he or she uses words. A writer's style depends on his or her word choice, sentence structure, figurative language, and sentence arrangement.
- **Purpose:** the reason an author decides to write about a specific topic. Then, once a topic is selected, the author must decide whether his or her purpose for writing is to inform, persuade, entertain, or explain his or her ideas to the reader.
- **Audience:** who the author is writing for; who will be reading the author's writing.
- **Graphic organizers:** diagrams or story maps that help a writer organize his or her ideas. There are many different types of graphic organizers for different types of writing.

The Writing Process

To produce a clear, well-developed, and organized writing piece, you should follow the steps in the writing process.

Expectations

☐ Develop and strengthen writing by planning, revising, and editing.

☐ Use prewriting strategies to formulate ideas.

☐ Know that a well-developed piece of writing requires more than one draft.

☐ Apply revision strategies.

☐ Edit your writing by checking for errors in capitalization, punctuation, grammar, and spelling.

☐ Prepare multiple drafts using revisions and edits to develop and strengthen your writing.

☐ Use technology to publish your writing.

Terms to Know

- **Writing process:** a step-by-step process that helps to produce a clear, well-developed, and organized piece of writing.

  o **Prewriting:** the first step in the writing process when a writer plans a piece of writing for the audience by brainstorming, researching, and gathering ideas.

  o **Drafting:** the next step in the writing process when a writer composes his or her ideas by writing down all of his or her ideas on paper in an organized way. A writer may write many drafts of a piece of writing to develop the topic with details for the audience.

  o **Revising:** the third step in the writing process when a writer rereads his or her piece of writing to improve it and make sure it will be clear for his or her audience. The writer adds, takes away, and reorganizes information.

  o **Editing:** the next step in the writing process when a writer proofreads and corrects errors in capitalization, punctuation, grammar, and spelling.

  o **Publishing:** the last step of the writing process when the final writing is shared with the audience.

Using the Writing Process

1. Planning	*This is a critical step!* • Choose a topic or analyze a prompt to set your purpose for writing. • Identify your audience. • Gather ideas by reading, researching, thinking, and taking notes. • Plan your writing by listing, drawing, or using a graphic organizer.
2. Drafting	• Use your plan to write your ideas. • Concentrate on organizing information logically and developing your topic with details for your audience and purpose. • Reread as you write.
3. Revising	• Reread and rewrite to make sure that your writing is clear. Ask yourself: o Will my writing make sense to my audience? o Are there any sentences I should reorganize to put the information in a better order? o Did I use enough details? o Is my writing organized? o Are there any words or phrases I could replace with more interesting ones?
4. Editing	• Reread and fix errors in your writing to get it ready for your audience. Check for correct: o capitalization o punctuation o spelling o use of language o format
5. Publishing	• Make a final copy—type or recopy. • Share with an audience. • Get feedback.

> If your writing is in response to a prompt about a text, there are a few steps to follow before you start the writing process. It is *very* important to first read the text closely, and then make sure that you understand what you are being asked to write about and who your audience will be. Once you have done this, follow the steps of the writing process for your response.

Researching

In fourth grade, you will have to do short research projects where you will have to investigate, or research, different parts of a topic. There will also be times that you will find information from different sources and put the information together into a piece of writing.

Expectations

- ☐ Focus research around a question/topic.
- ☐ Gather a variety of information about your research topic from print and digital sources.
- ☐ Take notes and organize information, and list the sources used.
- ☐ Sort the information from notes into provided categories.
- ☐ Prepare a list of sources used during research.
- ☐ Determine textual evidence that supports the analysis, reflection, and/or research.
- ☐ Compose written responses, and include textual evidence to strengthen the analysis, reflection, and/or research.
- ☐ Choose the writing structure to fit your task, purpose, and/or audience.

Terms to Know

- **Research:** the careful investigation and collection of information about a topic.
- **Source:** something that is used to find information about a topic.
  - o **Print sources:** books, newspaper articles, magazine articles
  - o **Digital sources:** websites, blogs, audio, video

- **Note taking:** writing down important information gathered from a source, making sure to not copy the author's words exactly. Jot down, in the form of a few words or a bulleted list, only important information located in a source, such as:

  o key words, including bold or italicized words.
  o main ideas.
  o important dates, people, and places.
  o repeated or emphasized information.
  o information from diagrams, charts, or illustrations.

- **Categories:** different groups of things or ideas into which you can sort research topic details.
- **Textual evidence:** evidence (information) from a fiction or nonfiction text that can be used to support your ideas in a piece of writing.

> Understanding how to use textual evidence is another really important skill to know to be successful on the Smarter Balanced assessments!

- **Analysis:** the process of studying and thinking about information.
- **Reflection:** thinking seriously and carefully about something.
- **Task:** a piece of work to be done that has specific directions.
- **Purpose:** the reason an author decides to write about a specific topic. Then, once a topic is selected, the author must decide whether his or her purpose for writing is to inform, persuade, entertain, or explain his or her ideas to the reader.
- **Audience:** who the author is writing for; who will be reading the author's writing.

Phew! You will need to know a lot to be successful on the English Language Arts section of the Smarter Balanced assessments! Remember, you have been working hard in school and have learned many things that will help you do well. Using the information in this book will help you too! Make sure to look back at this chapter for information if you need help understanding a term or what a question is asking you to do on the English Language Arts section of the Smarter Balanced assessments.

Preparing for the Computer-Adaptive Test

Overview

This chapter gives an overview of the English Language Arts Computer-Adaptive Test and shows you strategies for answering CAT questions with guided practice.

The English Language Arts Computer-Adaptive Test (ELA CAT) section of the Smarter Balanced assessments is a set of questions that measure your knowledge and skills with analytical reading. **Analytical reading** is a fancy way of saying that a reader reads a piece of text closely (very carefully with lots of thinking while reading), and then breaks down what he or she read in order to understand the messages or goals in the text. Analytic reading includes understanding the details you read, building knowledge, identifying words and phrases, figuring out the author's purpose, paying attention to how the text is set up, and connecting your thoughts to what you read.

ELA CAT items might ask the following to see how well you think while reading:

- Determine or summarize the main idea or key points of a text.
- Determine or summarize a theme (the "life lesson") of a text.
- Analyze characters' actions in the text.
- Analyze why the author wrote the text in a certain order.
- Compare information in a text.
- Choose the best beginning/ending for a story or write an introduction/ conclusion for a report.
- Analyze why an author chose certain words.
- Interpret the meaning of figurative language that the author used.
- Determine the meaning of a word using other information in the text.
- Identify spelling, punctuation, or grammar errors in a text.

Throughout the CAT questions, you will need to be able to *make an inference*. An **inference** is when you make a decision based on an experience—what you see, hear, or read. When you *make an inference*, you use "clues" an author or video gives you to figure out what the text or video is about. For example, read the following sentence and think about what inference you could make:

> *One Monday morning, Kelly rushed toward the end of her driveway, struggling to put on her backpack and yelling to the driver who was pulling away, "Wait for me!"*

If you answered that Kelly was running late to catch the school bus, you have just made an inference! The text did not say that exactly, but you used details from the text to make a decision—you made an inference.

For the ELA CAT section of the Smarter Balanced assessments, you will probably have four pieces of text to read with four or five questions for each text. You will also probably have four videos or audios with two or three questions for each. You will answer the questions about the texts or videos/audios in three ways:

1. selecting from multiple-choice answers.
2. typing a constructed response (developing a short answer to a question—a paragraph or two—which is sometimes called a "Brief Write"), including details from the text that support your answer.
3. using a technology-enhanced response to select a word or sentence by clicking to highlight or dragging and dropping.

Make sure to look back at Chapter 3 if you are unsure of the skills or terms in the questions on the practice test.

Guided Practice

In the next section of this chapter, you will learn strategies for answering the different types of questions on the ELA CAT and will have some guided practice questions. All of the practice questions will use the following myth, *Crow Brings Daylight*. Read it closely before going on.

Crow Brings Daylight

An Inuit Myth
retold by S. E. Schlosser

Long, long ago, when the world was still new, the Inuit lived in darkness in their home in the vastness of the north. They had never heard of daylight, and when it was first explained to them by Crow, who traveled back and forth between the northlands and the south, they did not believe him.

Yet many of the younger folk were fascinated by the story of the light that gilded the lands to the south. They made Crow repeat his tales until they knew them by heart.

"Imagine how far and how long we could hunt," they told one another.

"Yes, and see the polar bear before it attacks," others agreed.

Soon the yearning for daylight was so strong that the Inuit people begged Crow to bring it to them. Crow shook his head. "I am too old," he told them. "The daylight is very far away. I can no longer go so far." But the pleadings of the people made him reconsider, and finally he agreed to make the long journey to the south.

Crow flew for many miles through the endless dark of the north. He grew weary many times, and almost turned back. But at last he saw a rim of light at the very edge of the horizon and knew that the daylight was close.

Crow strained his wings and flew with all his might. Suddenly, the daylight world burst upon him with all its glory and brilliance. The endless shades of color and the many shapes and forms surrounding him made Crow stare and stare. He flapped down to a tree and rested himself, exhausted by his long journey. Above him, the sky was an endless blue, the clouds fluffy and white. Crow could not get enough of the wonderful scene.

Eventually Crow lowered his gaze and realized that he was near a village that lay beside a wide river. As he watched, a beautiful girl came to the river near the tree in which he perched. She dipped a large bucket into the icy waters of the river and then turned to make her way back to the village. Crow turned himself into a tiny speck of dust and drifted down towards the girl as she passed beneath his tree. He settled into her fur cloak and watched carefully as she returned to the snow lodge of her father, who was the chief of the village people.

It was warm and cozy inside the lodge. Crow looked around him and spotted a box that glowed around the edges. Daylight, he thought. On the floor, a little boy was playing contentedly. The speck of dust that was Crow drifted away from the girl and floated into the ear of the little boy. Immediately the child sat up and rubbed at his ear, which was irritated by the strange speck. He started to cry, and the chief, who was a doting grandfather, came running into the snow lodge to see what was wrong.

"Why are you crying?" the chief asked, kneeling beside the child.

Inside the little boy's ear, Crow whispered: "You want to play with a ball of daylight." The little boy rubbed at his ear and then repeated Crow's words. The chief sent his daughter to the glowing box in the corner. She brought it to her father, who removed a glowing ball, tied it with a string, and gave it to the little boy. He rubbed his ear thoughtfully before taking the ball. It was full of light and shadow, color and form. The child laughed happily, tugging at the string and watching the ball bounce.

Then Crow scratched the inside of his ear again and the little boy gasped and cried.

"Don't cry, little one," said the doting grandfather anxiously. "Tell me what is wrong."

Inside the boy's ear, Crow whispered: "You want to go outside to play." The boy rubbed at his ear and then repeated Crow's words to his grandfather. Immediately, the chief lifted up the small child and carried him outside, followed by his worried mother.

As soon as they were free of the snow lodge, Crow swooped out of the child's ear and resumed his natural form. He dove toward the little boy's hand and grabbed the string from him. Then he rose up and up into the endless blue sky, the ball of daylight sailing along behind him.

In the far north, the Inuit saw a spark of light coming toward them through the darkness. It grew brighter and brighter, until they could see Crow flapping his wings as he flew toward them. The people gasped and pointed and called in delight. The Crow dropped the ball, and it shattered upon the ground, releasing the daylight so that it exploded up and out, illuminating every dark place and chasing away every shadow. The sky grew bright and turned blue. The dark mountains took on color and light and form. The snow and ice sparkled so brightly that the Inuit had to shade their eyes.

The people laughed and cried and exclaimed over their good fortune. But Crow told them that the daylight would not last forever. He had only obtained one ball of daylight from the people of the south, and it would need to rest for six months every year to regain its strength. During that six month period, the darkness would return.

The people said: "Half a year of daylight is enough. Before you brought the daylight, we lived our whole life in darkness!" Then they thanked Crow over and over again.

To this day, the Inuit live for half a year in darkness and half a year in daylight. And they are always kind to Crow, for it was he who brought them the light.

Strategies for Answering Questions with Multiple-Choice Answers

The questions with multiple-choice answers will usually include a short amount of text for you to read, a question about the text, and the three to five options from which you will choose only one answer.

To answer a multiple-choice question, follow these steps:

1. Read the entire passage closely. Be sure to think while you read so that you understand what the passage is about. When you have finished, skim back over the passage to make sure you understand the main idea.
2. Read the question carefully to understand what is being asked.
3. Come up with an answer in your head before you look at the answer choices. This way, some of the answer choices given will not throw you off or trick you.
4. Look back into the passage to find or check information that supports your answer.
5. Read ALL of the answer choices.
6. Eliminate the answers you know are not right, looking for the one that answers the question BEST.
7. Look back in the passage to double-check the information that supports the answer you chose.

A NOTE ABOUT QUESTIONS WITH MULTIPLE-CHOICE ANSWERS ON THE CAT

Some of the questions with multiple-choice answers will be two-part questions. The first part will ask a question where you will have to think about the text and make a decision, such as *What inference can be made about . . .* The next part will ask you to choose a sentence from the text that best supports the decision you made.

Guided Practice: Questions with Multiple-Choice Answers

Practice Question 1

Read the following sentence from the passage. Then, answer the question.

"Crow <u>strained</u> his wings and flew with all his might."

What does the use of the word <u>strained</u> *most likely* mean?

- O A. flapped quickly
- O B. cleaned
- O C. flapped powerfully
- O D. rested

Answer: (C)

Explanation: To help figure out this answer, you need to look for clues in the words surrounding "strained." For example, the previous paragraph states that "Crow flew for many miles through the endless dark of the north. He grew weary many times, and almost turned back. But at last he saw a rim of light at the very edge of the horizon and knew that the daylight was close." Also, the last part of the sentence in this question states that Crow "flew with all his might." Both of these quotes give clues that Crow was using all of his energy to fly. Choice A may make sense, but if Crow were flying with "all his might," Choice C is a better answer. Choices B and D do not make sense in the plot.

Scoring Rubric: 1 point if the correct response is selected.

Practice Question 2

Which sentence **best** describes why the younger folk made Crow repeat his tales of the light until they knew them by heart?

- O A. The younger folk liked Crow's storytelling skills.
- O B. The younger folk enjoyed listening to stories about daylight.
- O C. The younger folk wanted to go to the lands of the south.
- O D. The younger folk had never heard of daylight, and they were fascinated by it.

Answer: (D)

Explanation: This is correct because these details are stated in the passage in the first and second paragraphs. Choices A, B, and C may be possible answers, but they are not supported by details in the text.

Scoring Rubric: 1 point if the correct response is selected.

Practice Question 3

The following question has two parts. First, answer Part A. Then, answer Part B.

Part A

Which of these inferences about Crow is supported by the text?

- O A. Crow resents daylight.
- O B. Crow wanted to bring daylight to the Inuit.
- O C. Crow liked the boy.
- O D. Crow is always honest.

Part B

Which sentence(s) from the passage **best** supports your answer to Part A? Select one option.

- O A. "They made Crow repeat his tales until they knew them by heart."
- O B. "Crow shook his head. 'I am too old,' he told them."
- O C. "Crow flew for many miles through the endless dark of the north."
- O D. "Then they thanked Crow over and over again."

Answer: Part A: (B)
         Part B: (C)

Explanation:

Part A: This is correct because details in the passage tell you that Crow decided to fly south for many miles even when he was tired, tricked the village people to get the ball of daylight, and then flew all the way back to the Inuit. This makes you think—or infer—that Crow wanted to bring daylight to the Inuit. There are no details in the passage to support the claims that Crow resented daylight or liked the boy. In addition, Crow was in fact dishonest, not honest, when he tricked the village people.

Part B: This is the only sentence that supports the answer to Part A.

Scoring Rubric: 1 point if the correct responses are selected for *both* Part A and Part B.

Strategies for Answering Questions with Constructed-Response Answers

What is a constructed response? A constructed response is a type of open-ended essay question that demonstrates knowledge and reasoning.

Constructed: *Construction* means to build something. *Constructed* means that something has been built.

Response: A *response* is an answer.

A constructed response to reading is when you "build" an answer to a question about a piece of text by writing about your thinking. Responding to a piece of text is not always about right and wrong answers. Many times there is more than one "right" answer or there are ways to make an answer "better." In order for your response to be a great response, you need to include more than just a simple answer—you need to explain your reasoning and use examples from the text to support your reasoning.

As with answering questions with multiple-choice answers, be sure to do the following:

1. Read the entire passage closely. Be sure to think while you read so that you understand what the passage is about. When you have finished, skim back over the passage to make sure you understand the main idea.

2. Read the question carefully to understand what is being asked.

3. Then, use the **R.A.C.E. strategy** to develop a well-crafted constructed response to questions about a text. The R.A.C.E. strategy is a method used to thoroughly answer a constructed-response question. Table 4-1 outlines the R.A.C.E. strategy.

Table 4-1. R.A.C.E. Strategy

R—Restate	First, **restate** the question to start your answer. To restate the question means that you put the question into a statement as a part of the answer you provide. For example: Question: What color is the sky? Answer: *The color of the sky is blue.* Question: Where did you go for vacation this year? Answer: *For vacation this year, I went to the beach.*
A—Answer	Then, **answer** the question. What is the question asking? Make sure you answer the question! The answer, as in the examples above, may come in the first sentence as you restate the question into a statement.
C—Cite	Next, go back to the text to look for and **cite** the evidence that best supports your answer. When you *cite evidence*, you use exact words or specific examples from the text that best support your answer. Identify where the answer is found. If you use someone else's exact words, you NEED to put them in quotation marks. You want to be selective about the evidence you choose to include in your response. Be sure to choose evidence that BEST supports your answer.
E—Explain	Finally, **explain** your reasoning: why you think your answer is right and how your evidence supports your answer. Use your background knowledge and experiences to build on your answer or extend your answer by making connections—text to self; text to text; or text to world. For example, your explanation may start off like: *I think this shows that . . .*

4. Reread your answer, and check each step of R.A.C.E. Make revisions, if needed, before moving on to the next question.

Guided Practice: Questions with Constructed-Response Answers

Practice Question 4

In *Crow Brings Daylight*, what inference can be made about how the grandfather feels about the boy? Support your answer with details from the text.

Answer and Explanation: Answers will vary. A sample response is provided below. This sample response describes an inference that can be made about how the grandfather feels about the boy and is supported with evidence from the passage. It follows the R.A.C.E. strategy framework. You would not actually write the names of the R.A.C.E. steps in your answer. They are written here just to help you see the framework.

Sample Response:

(RESTATE) An inference that can be made about how the grandfather feels about the boy is that (ANSWER) he cares about the boy. (CITE) In the passage, when the boy cries, the grandfather runs into the lodge, kneels beside the boy, and asks him what's wrong. When the boy said he wanted to play with the ball of daylight, the grandfather let him. (EXPLAIN) I think this shows that the grandfather likes the boy.

Scoring Rubric

2 points	A response that
	• gives sufficient evidence of the ability to make a clear inference.
	• includes specific examples/details that make clear reference to the text.
	• adequately explains the inference with clearly relevant information based on the text.
1 point	A response that
	• gives limited evidence of the ability to make an inference.
	• includes vague/limited examples/details that make reference to the text.
	• explains an inference with vague/limited information based on the text.
0 points	A response that
	• gives no evidence of the ability to make an inference.
	OR
	• gives an inference but includes no examples/details that make reference to the text.
	OR
	• gives an inference but includes no explanation or no relevant information from the text.

Strategies for Answering Questions with Technology-Enhanced Response Answers

You will have some questions on your ELA CAT that will require you to give a technology-enhanced response. Remember, you will be taking the Smarter Balanced assessments on the computer. These types of questions may ask you to click to highlight a word or sentence or to drag and drop a word or sentence to match specific questions.

As with answering the other question types, be sure to do the following:

1. Read the entire passage closely. Be sure to think while you read so that you understand what the passage is about. When you have finished, skim back over the passage to make sure you understand the main idea.

2. Read the question carefully to understand what is being asked.

(Are you figuring out that these two steps are super important?)

These types of questions will mostly involve vocabulary—the meaning of words. Look back at a specific word in the text and "read around the word." This means that you need to look at the sentence before, the sentence the word is in, and the sentence after the word to find hints about what the word means.

Guided Practice: Questions with Technology-Enhanced Response Answers

Practice Question 5

Read this part of the text again.

"The Crow dropped the ball, and it shattered upon the ground, releasing the daylight so that it exploded up and out, illuminating every dark place and chasing away every shadow. The sky grew bright and turned blue. The dark mountains took on color and light and form. The snow and ice sparkled so brightly that the Inuit had to shade their eyes."

Click on two words that are synonyms for "break apart."

Answer and Explanation

Answer: shattered and **exploded**

Explanation: Both of these words mean "break apart." (Of course, on this practice question, you could not actually click on the words. You'll have to wait to take the test on the computer at school to actually click!)

Scoring Rubric: 1 point if the two correct responses are made.

Preparing for the Performance Task

Overview

This chapter will give an overview of the English Language Arts Performance Task, and introduce you to strategies for responding to the ELA Performance Task.

The English Language Arts Performance Task (ELA PT) section of the Smarter Balanced assessments is a set of questions and an activity that measures how you use and apply your critical-thinking and problem-solving skills.

A performance task is a type of assessment that will ask you to demonstrate your skills and thinking as you read and write about a real-world situation.

> **Performance** = the action or process of carrying out or accomplishing an action or task

> **Task** = a piece of work to be done; a job

Therefore, a performance task could also be described as a process that you go through to complete a piece of work.

The ELA Performance Task will ask you to complete a piece of work connected to a single, real-world topic or scenario (situation). After learning and reading about the topic, you will answer three or four questions about your research. For the main part of the Performance Task, you will respond to a writing prompt by writing an extended response (a full-length piece of writing) about the task's scenario.

Real-world scenarios for an ELA PT might be:

- A magazine for fourth graders has asked you to write a folktale for the magazine! Research folktales by reading an information article about folktales and two actual folktales. *Write a folktale* using the information you have read.

- Your class is learning about the groups of people that traveled west in the 1880s and will be creating displays to show what you have learned. Your teacher wants each student to write an informational article about the struggles people faced during the westward movement that will be displayed with your project. Complete research for your informational article by reading two articles and viewing a video about the westward movement. *Write an informational article* using the information you read/viewed.
- Your animal club at school is deciding whether or not to participate in a project with a local zoo. You have been chosen to write an opinion essay for the club's newsletter on whether zoos are good for animals. Complete research to form your opinion by reading two articles and watching a video about animals in zoos. *Write an opinion essay* using information that you read/viewed.

The Smarter Balanced ELA Performance Task requires you to be involved in three sections:

1. Participating in a classroom activity
2. Reading, viewing, and/or listening to information and taking notes on the sources (information) presented and answering questions about the sources
3. Writing an extended response to the situation presented

Classroom Activity

The ELA PT begins with a classroom activity that your teacher will present to you and your classmates. The activity will happen in your classroom at some point before you do the computer part of the Performance Task. Your teacher will lead a 30-minute discussion, which will give you an introduction for the task's topic. He or she may read aloud, show a video, or create a chart of information about the topic. The classroom activity will be like a "warm up" for the Performance Task. It will help prepare you for the Performance Task by providing background information and key vocabulary, but it will not give you a description of the actual task that you will complete.

Performance Task

You will complete the performance task on your own using a computer. There are two parts to the performance task as outlined below.

Part 1

- This part is approximately 35 minutes.
- You will be expected to:

  o   read the directions and the steps to follow in order to complete your task.

  o   read and/or view three sources related to the task.

  o   take notes on the information you learn from the sources to help you with your writing task.

  o   answer three or four questions about the sources you have read.

Part 2

- This part is approximately 70 minutes.
- You will be expected to:

  o   read the directions for your assignment.

  o   read how your written task will be scored.

  o   review your notes and the sources from Part 1.

  o   write a response for your task, using evidence from the sources, and by planning, drafting, and revising your writing.

Unlike the ELA CAT, the work you do on the computer for the ELA PT is not adaptive (not adjusted to be easier or more challenging based on your answers to previous questions). You and all of your classmates will, however, have access to the following electronic universal tools that may be helpful for the ELA PT:

- **Digital Notepad:** This tool is for making notes about an item.
- **Expandable Passages:** Each passage can be expanded so that it takes up a larger portion of the screen.
- **Global Notes** (only available for the ELA PT): This is a notepad where your notes are kept from Part 1 to Part 2 of the PT. (You could also use scratch paper.)
- **Highlighter:** This feature allows you to mark desired text with color.
- **Spell Checker:** This feature will underline words that you have spelled incorrectly, but it will not provide the correct spelling. You will have to choose the correct spelling from a drop-down list.
- **Writing Tools:** These include bold, italics, bullets, and undo/redo.

Depending on your learning style, your school may make other designated supports or accommodations available to you to assist you with showing your work.

The Smarter Balanced Performance Task for fourth graders will require you to complete *one* of three types of writing:

1. **Narrative Writing.** For narrative writing, you develop real or imagined experiences or events using descriptive details and clear event sequences—a story. The real-life scenario about folktales is an example of when you would have to use narrative writing for an ELA Performance Task.

2. **Information Writing.** For information writing, you tell factual information about a topic, making sure to convey your ideas and information clearly. The real-life scenario about the westward movement is an example of when you would have to use information writing for an ELA Performance Task.

3. **Opinion Writing.** For opinion writing, you will write your opinion on topics or texts and support your point of view with reasons and information. The real-life scenario about animals in zoos is an example of when you would have to use opinion writing for an ELA Performance Task.

Guided Practice

Now, let's review strategies for thinking about and answering the different sections on the ELA PT.

Before reading the following strategies, now is a good time to go back to Chapter 3 and review the "Types of Texts," "Writing," and "Researching" sections. These sections will be *very helpful* for completing an effective performance task.

Below are 8 key strategies to review and practice when preparing for the ELA PT:

1. **Pay close attention during the classroom activity.**

   - The purpose of the classroom activity is to increase your understanding of the topic that will be part of the Performance Task and to prepare you for the type of thinking and writing you will have to do for it.
   - Listen carefully to your teacher's presentation, and ask questions if you do not understand the ideas or vocabulary.

2. **Understand what the writing task is asking you to do.**

   - When you start the Performance Task on the computer, read all of the directions first. Read the description of your task. Make sure you understand what you are being asked to do. Put yourself into the scenario, and approach the work that you are being asked to do as if it were a real job for you.

3. **Read and/or view the sources carefully.**

   - As you read/view each of the three sources, stop frequently to make sure you understand what you are reading. You need to understand the main idea of each source as well as the specific details.
   - Take notes on each source. Most people take notes by making lists of important details for each source. Important information would include

     o   key words, including bold or italicized words
     o   main ideas
     o   important dates, people, places
     o   repeated or emphasized information
     o   information from diagrams, charts, or illustrations

   - You can take notes using the Global Notes on the computer or using scratch paper. During Part 2 of the PT, you will be able to use the notes you wrote in Part 1.
   - When you are working on the written response, look back at your notes for details or to help find information to add to your writing.

4. **Look back into the sources for information.**

   - This is important for answering the research questions.
   - When you are preparing your written response, using *textual evidence* is really important in order to be successful on this test! Remember, textual evidence is information from a source that can be used to support your ideas in a piece of writing.

5. Focus on the format for the type of writing you are being asked to do.

- For all types of writing, it is important to know who will be reading your writing. Make sure you know who your audience will be. Use a writing style (word choice, sentence structure, figurative language, and sentence arrangement) that will help your audience understand.

- If you are asked to write a narrative, include the setting, characters, events in the plot, and a conclusion. Use the sources to help guide your writing.

- If you are asked to write an information essay, include an introduction about the topic, a few paragraphs about facts related to the topic, and a conclusion. Include details from the sources.

- If you are asked to write an opinion essay, include an introduction describing the topic and stating your opinion, a few paragraphs with reasons for your opinion and examples to support your opinion, and a conclusion. Include details from the sources.

6. Develop the topic of information and opinion writing with examples from the sources.

- Develop your topic by using evidence from the text to support your thinking.

- When you use evidence from a text, it is called "citing" the text. Sentence starters for citing a text in your writing include

  o *The author says . . .*
  o *The author wrote . . .*
  o *Based on what I read . . ..*
  o *The illustration shows . . .*
  o *On page 00, the author said . . .*
  o *In paragraph 00, the author wrote . . .*

7. Understand how your writing will be scored.

- Each Performance Task will tell you how your work will be scored. Read this section carefully, and use it to guide you as you make decisions about your writing.

- Look back at the scoring information when you think you have finished your written response. Make revisions to your writing to help match it to the expectations.

8. Use the Writing Process as outlined in Table 5-1 below.

Table 5-1. Writing Process

1. Planning	This is a critical step! • Choose a topic or analyze a prompt to set the purpose for your writing. • Identify your audience. • Gather ideas by reading, researching, thinking, and taking notes. • Plan your writing by listing, drawing, or using a graphic organizer.
2. Drafting	• Use your plan to write your ideas. • Concentrate on organizing information logically and developing your topic with details for your audience and purpose. • Reread as you write.

3. Revising	• Reread and rewrite to make sure that your writing is clear. Ask yourself:
	
	  o Will my writing make sense to my audience?
	  o Are there any sentences I should reorganize to put the information in a better order?
	  o Did I use enough details?
	  o Is my writing organized?
	  o Are there any words or phrases I could replace with more interesting ones?

4. Editing	• Reread and fix up errors in your writing to get it ready for your audience. Check for correct:
	
	  o capitalization
	  o punctuation
	  o spelling
	  o use of language
	  o format

5. Publishing	• Make a final copy—type or recopy.

English Language Arts Practice Test

Computer-Adaptive Test

> ### NOTE
>
> On the actual exam, the format for longer text passages and questions will be different. Text passages, and the questions that accompany them, will be placed in a side-by-side scrollable format. This side-by-side format will allow you to easily refer back to the passage for textual evidence.

Directions: For Questions 1–4, read *How the Chipmunk Got Its Stripes*. Then, answer the questions.

How the Chipmunk Got Its Stripes

An Animal Tale

Long ago, the porcupine was chosen head chief of all the animals. That was when the animals had chiefs and tribes like the Indians. He was made head chief, because nothing could hurt him.

One day, when he was roaming through the forest, he heard the animals roaring and growling. He stopped to hear what they were saying.

"Always night! Always night!" growled some of the animals.

"Let us have daylight all of the time, daylight all the time!" roared the others.

"How can I settle the matter?" said he to himself. "I know what I will do. I will call a council of all the animals and let them decide."

So that night he called a council of all the animals. From north, south, east, and west they came. They built a blazing fire in the forest and seated themselves in a ring around it. Some were stern and serious, while others looked fierce and threatening. The porcupine seemed very worried as he rose to address them.

"I cannot decide," said he, "whether we shall have daylight all the time or darkness all the time."

There was a great commotion. All the animals talked at once. They roared and growled so that no one could hear what they were saying. But above them all the bear's big deep voice rumbled out. Rocking to and fro on his hind legs, he growled, "Always night! Always night! Always night for me!"

Just outside the ring a little chipmunk squeaked out, "The light will come! The light will come!"

The other animals paid no attention to the little creature, but kept on roaring and growling. The little chipmunk laughed to himself and danced around and around, shrieking, "The light will come! They light will come!"

Suddenly a faint light spread over the eastern sky and the round disk of the sun rose above the horizon. Daylight had come. Silence fell on the astonished group.

"Could it be possible that daylight would come whether they wanted to or not?"

"What did I tell you?" squeaked the little chipmunk, as he darted away into the forest.

The angry bear ran after him, but the little creature was too quick for him. The chipmunk ran to his home in the hollow tree, but, just as he entered the hole, the clumsy bear struck him with his paw. His claws made black stripes on the chipmunk's back, and there they are to this day.

1. Reread the following sentence from the passage. Then, answer the question.

   "Some were <u>stern</u> and serious, while others looked fierce and threatening."

   What does the use of the word <u>stern</u> *most likely* mean?

   - O A. soft
   - O B. angry
   - O C. mean
   - O D. unsmiling

2. How is the chipmunk different from the other animals?

   - O A. The chipmunk was afraid of the darkness.
   - O B. The chipmunk knew that the day would come no matter what.
   - O C. The chipmunk was angry about the light.
   - O D. The chipmunk was the largest animal in the forest.

3. The following question has two parts. First, answer Part A. Then, answer Part B.

   Part A: Which one of these inferences about the porcupine is supported by the text?

   - O A. The porcupine was a dull leader.
   - O B. The porcupine was a fair leader.
   - O C. The porcupine was a bad leader.
   - O D. The porcupine was a happy leader.

   Part B: Which sentence from the passage *best* supports your answer to Part A?

   - O A. "The porcupine was chosen head chief of all the animals."
   - O B. "One day, when he was roaming through the forest, he heard the animals roaring and growling."
   - O C. "He stopped to hear what they were saying."
   - O D. "'I will call a council of all the animals and let them decide.'"

4. In a few sentences, summarize how the tale explains why chipmunks have black stripes on their backs. Use details from the story to support your answer. Write your answer in the box below.

Directions: For Questions 5—8, read *A Look at Spiders*. Then, answer the questions.

A Look at Spiders

What Is a Spider?

Spiders are unique creatures! Many people think that spiders are insects, but they are not. To the untrained eye they may look alike, but they have many differences. Spiders have two main body parts, eight legs, and no wings. Insects have three main body parts, six legs, and usually do have wings. Spiders have piercing jaws, while insects have jaws that chew. All spiders can make silk thread (although not all spiders spin webs), but most insects cannot. Spiders cannot fly whereas many insects have wings allowing them to do so.

How Big Are Spiders?

Spiders come in many sizes. The largest spider in the world is the Giant Bird-eating spider. The largest one found had a leg span as big as a dinner plate! The smallest spider is the Patu Marplesi. You could fit 10 of them on the end of a pencil. Female spiders are always larger than male spiders.

Where Do Spiders Live?

Spiders live in many places. They are found all over the world in all sorts of habitats from the seashore to the desert. They can live on the ground, under rocks, on plants, in trees, in caves, and on water.

What and How Do Spiders Eat?

Spiders spend most of their lives searching for food. All spiders are carnivores, which means they eat mainly meat. Most spiders eat insects, but a few of the larger species are big enough to prey on small animals like mice or lizards.

Spiders have a strange way of eating. Because spiders cannot chew, they inject venom through their fangs and paralyze their victims. The poison turns the insides of the insect to liquid and the spider sucks it up. It is like drinking milk through a straw!

How Do Spiders Make Silk?

Spiders have special glands in the back part of their bodies. These glands, called spinnerets, make silk. All spiders spin silk, but not all spiders spin webs. The spider's body has an oil on it to keep the spider from sticking to its own web. Silk is used for climbing, to create webs, build egg sacs, and wrap prey.

Can Spiders Harm People?

The majority of spiders are harmless to humans. Most spider poison will not harm people, because it is quite weak. The feared tarantula is not poisonous. A tarantula's bite can be painful, but it isn't any more dangerous than a bee sting. In fact, spiders are helpful to humans. They pollinate plants and eat many types of destructive insects, keeping gardens free of pests.

5. How is the last paragraph different from the ones that come before it in the passage?

   O A. It describes what spiders eat, whereas the other paragraphs describe what eats spiders.

   O B. It helps the reader understand that most spiders are not harmful, whereas the other paragraphs help the reader understand details about spiders.

   O C. It helps the reader understand where spiders live, whereas the other paragraphs help the reader understand what spiders eat.

   O D. It describes how spiders are similar to insects, whereas the other paragraphs describe different sizes of spiders.

6. What was the author's purpose in paragraph 1?

   O A. to tell the reader that spiders and insects look alike

   O B. to explain to the reader how spiders and insects are different

   O C. to persuade the reader that spiders are better than insects

   O D. to describe to the reader a spider's body

7. Reread the following sentence from the passage. Then, answer the question.

"Spiders have <u>piercing</u> jaws, while insects have jaws that chew."

What does the use of the word <u>piercing</u> *most likely* mean?

- ○ A. biting
- ○ B. strong
- ○ C. weak
- ○ D. grinding

8. You have been asked to write a summary of this passage. Choose **three** key details from the passage that you would use in your summary.

- ☐ A. "Spiders cannot fly, whereas many insects have wings allowing them to do so."
- ☐ B. "Spiders come in many sizes."
- ☐ C. "These glands, called spinnerets, make silk."
- ☐ D. "The majority of spiders are harmless to humans."
- ☐ E. "Spiders have a strange way of eating."
- ☐ F. "The spider's body has an oil on it to keep the spider from sticking to its own web."

Directions: For Question 9, read *The Crow and the Pitcher*. Then, answer the question.

The Crow and the Pitcher

It was a sweltering hot day. A crow, parched with thirst, came upon a pitcher of water. But the pitcher was only half full. The crow leaned and stretched and thrust out his beak as far as he could. No matter how hard he tried, he could not reach the water.

All of a sudden, the crow had an idea. He picked up a pebble in his beak and dropped it in the water. The water level in the pitcher rose just a tiny bit. So he dropped in another pebble, then another, then one more. The crow continued doing this for a long time. Finally, the water in the pitcher had risen enough. The crow poked his beak in and drank to his heart's content.

9. In a few sentences, explain what lesson the reader can learn from the crow. Use details from the story to support your answer. Write your answer in the box below.

Directions: For Question 10, read "Bed in Summer." Then, answer the prompt that follows.

Bed in Summer

by Robert Louis Stevenson

In winter I get up at night
And dress by yellow candle-light.
In summer, quite the other way,
I have to go to bed by day.

I have to go to bed and see
The birds still hopping on the tree,
Or hear the grown-up people's feet
Still going past me in the street.

And does it not seem hard to you,
When all the sky is clear and blue,
And I should like so much to play,
To have to go to bed by day?

10. Explain why the author of the poem does not like going to bed in the summer. Use details from the poem to support your response. Write your answer in the box below.

Directions: For Questions 11 and 12, read the following text that contains an astronaut's diary entries. Then, answer the questions.

July 6: Our space shuttle will get to the space station tomorrow. I am looking forward to meeting the other astronauts. There is a lot of interesting work to do. We have been working hard to prepare for our arrival, and we are exhausted. Not only is there so much to do, one of us has to be awake all the time. We have to sleep in shifts.

July 7: Finally, we got to our destination. We reached the space station! The six astronauts on the space station were happy to see us. They said, "We have been waiting for you!" We were glad to see them too. There will be more work to do here, but there will be less pressure. There will be more people to help us. We will be able to share the work.

Our first night on the space station was great! We completed some important work together and then had a good dinner. When we were done with dinner, the captain of the space shuttle said each person would have to take turns staying awake. We were going to have to sleep in shifts again!

When the captain gave us the schedule, I saw that I was first. I was disappointed. I had already been awake for 20 hours, and I was very fatigued. But I knew it was my duty to stay awake. I sighed and said to the others, "See you in the morning."

I became an astronaut so that I could travel in space. Now that I am here, I realize how much hard work there is to do! It's even more challenging than I expected.

11. The following question has two parts. First, answer Part A. Then, answer Part B.

    Part A: What inference can you make about the narrator in this diary entry?

    ○ A. The narrator likes to sleep.
    ○ B. The narrator did not realize that being an astronaut was such a hard job.
    ○ C. The narrator is not happy to be an astronaut.
    ○ D. The narrator does not like to work.

    Part B: Which sentence from the passage *best* supports your answer to Part A?

    ○ A. "When the captain gave us the schedule, I saw that I was first."
    ○ B. "I became an astronaut so that I could travel in space. Now that I am here, I realize how much hard work there is to do!"
    ○ C. "The six astronauts on the space station were happy to see us."
    ○ D. "'Finally, we got to our destination."

12. Reread the following sentence from the passage. Then, answer the question.

    "I had already been awake for 20 hours, and I was very fatigued. But I knew it was my duty to stay awake."

    What does the use of the word fatigued *most likely* mean?

    ○ A. weak
    ○ B. tired
    ○ C. hungry
    ○ D. large

Directions: For Question 13, read the passage entitled *Gabby Douglas*. Then, answer the question.

Gabby Douglas

Gabby Douglas was born in Virginia Beach, Virginia, on December 30, 1995. She has three siblings. Her first experience with gymnastics came at the age of 3 when she perfected a straight cartwheel that she learned from her older sister. She began formal gymnastics training at 6 years old and won a state championship by the time she was 8. She moved away from her hometown and family in 2010 to pursue training with a world-renowned Olympic trainer.

Douglas was selected to compete with the U.S. Olympic women's gymnastics team at the 2012 Summer Olympics. There, she became the first African American to win gold in the individual all-around event. She was 16 years old. She also won a team gold medal with her teammates.

Thanks to her high-flying feats on the uneven bars, her best gymnastic event, Douglas was nicknamed the "Flying Squirrel."

13. Write a summary of key events that led to Gabby Douglas becoming a successful gymnast. Use details from the passage in your summary to support your answer. Write your answer in the box below.

Directions: For Question 14, read the paragraph. Then, answer the question.

The rain had finally stopped, and the sun was starting to peek through the clouds. My brother and I took a walk around the neighborhood to splash in the leftover puddles. As the sun shone brighter, we looked toward the sky at the end of our street and smiled at the sight of a rainbow. The rainbow we saw <u>was nice</u>. We watched it in amazement for a few minutes. Soon, it disappeared as the sky turned bright blue.

14. Revise this paragraph by choosing the phrase with the **best** descriptive detail to replace <u>was nice</u>.

   O A. shone because it had been raining
   O B. looked bigger than the one we saw before
   O C. had a lot of colors
   O D. sparkled with arched stripes of color

Directions: For Question 15, read the paragraph. Then, answer the question.

A soap bubble is a very thin film of soapy water. When soap and water are mixed together and air is blown into the mixture, the soap forms a thin skin or wall and traps the air to create a bubble. Soap bubbles usually last for only a few seconds before they <u>break</u> when coming into contact with another object.

15. Choose a word to replace <u>break</u> that better describes what happens to a bubble when it comes into contact with another object.

   O A. bounce
   O B. burst
   O C. disappear
   O D. float

Directions: For Question 16, read the paragraph. Then, answer the question.

Like humans, dogs use their noses to smell. But dogs have a sense of smell that is said to be a thousand times more sensitive than that of humans. Dogs rely on their sense of smell to understand their world. _____ noses make them the perfect helper for search and rescue teams looking for missing persons.

16. Choose the correct word to fill in the blank.

    ○ A. Dog's
    ○ B. Dogs
    ○ C. Dogs'
    ○ D. Dogses

Directions: For Question 17, read *Thomas Edison's Early Years*. Then, answer the question.

Thomas Edison's Early Years

Thomas Alva Edison was born February 11, 1847, in Milan, Ohio. In 1854, when he was seven, the family moved to Michigan, where Edison spent the rest of his childhood.

He was nicknamed "Al" at an early age and went to school only a short time. He did so poorly that his mother, a former teacher, taught her son at home. Al learned to love reading, a habit he kept for the rest of his life. Young Edison set up a chemical laboratory in the cellar of their large house, where he liked to make experiments.

At the age of 12, Edison sold fruit, snacks, and newspapers on a train. He even printed his own newspaper, the *Grand Trunk Herald*. At 16, he roamed the country working as a telegrapher. The telegraph was the first electric long distance communication system, and a telegrapher used a kind of alphabet called Morse Code to send and receive messages over the telegraph. In his spare time, he took things apart to see how they worked. Finally, he decided to invent things himself.

In his 20s, Edison moved to New York City, where he invented and patented his first invention, the electric vote recorder. It was a failure. He got his big break in 1870 when he invented an improved stock ticker for the stock exchange. He went on to become a full-time inventor and invented 1,093 inventions. His most famous inventions include the phonograph and light bulb. When people called him a genius, he would answer, "Genius is hard work, stick-to-it-iveness, and common sense."

17. Explain the author's *most likely* purpose for writing about Thomas Edison as a child and a young man. Use examples from the passage to support your response. Write your answer in the box below.

Directions: For Question 18, read the following draft of a report, about a recent class trip to a zoo, that a student is writing for her teacher. Then, answer the question.

Our day at the zoo started at the African area. We saw giraffes with long, slender necks that made them tall enough to eat leaves from the tree tops. We saw one-humped camels. Camels are called "ships of the deserts" because camels are able to carry people across deserts just like ships that carry people across an ocean. We saw zebras with their special black and white striped coats.

Our second stop was the bird aviary. The aviary was like a giant cage and had over 40 types of birds. We saw many colorful parrots, different kinds of pigeons, and proud eagles. That part of the zoo was very noisy! We enjoyed the birds the most.

18. Write an introduction, in the box below, that clearly states the main idea of this report and sets up the information to come in the body of the report.

Directions: For Question 19, a student has written a draft of an opinion letter to his school librarian about students being allowed to sign out only two books per week from the library at a time. The student wants to revise the draft to add more support for his opinion. Read the draft of the letter, and then answer the question.

Dear Mrs. Vance,

I am writing to ask you to allow students to sign out more than two books at a time from the library. Two books per week is not enough for students to get the most out of reading. We often finish reading the two books before the end of the week. If we finish reading the two books, we have nothing new and interesting to read until we come to the library the next week. Also, getting books from the library is the only way we can read to gather research ideas for reports we have to write for class. Being able to sign out more than two books would make us happier and better readers and writers.

Sincerely,

Abe Mesh

19. Choose **two** sentences that *best* support the underlined portion of the letter.

☐ A. If we could sign out more than two books, we would look smarter.

☐ B. In my cousin's school, students can sign out four books each week.

☐ C. If we could sign out more than two books, we could spend more time reading at home.

☐ D. Another problem is that the library's computers are always being used by other students.

☐ E. Most students like to read mysteries and books about sports.

☐ F. Students who are able to take out more than two books from the library will be more knowledgeable about things they need to learn for school.

Directions: For Question 20, a student is writing in his reading journal, describing an exciting part of a book that he is reading to his teacher. Read his journal entry, and then answer the question.

An exciting part in my book was when the main character, Kenneth, went to the lake to try to catch some fish for his mother to cook for lunch. He cast his fishing line into the water for an hour with no luck. Suddenly, he saw a woman tip over in her canoe in the middle of the lake. She was not wearing a life jacket and was <u>asking</u> for help. Kenneth ran to a nearby house to get help. His actions helped save the woman's life.

20. The student has decided to replace the underlined word to make his meaning clearer. Which word would be a *better* choice?

   O A. yelling
   O B. demanding
   O C. begging
   O D. calling

Directions: For Question 21, a student is writing a report on rocks. She needs to correct the punctuation and grammar usage mistakes in her report. Read the paragraph from the draft of her report. Then answer the question.

One type of rock is called an igneous rock. An igneous rock is formed when magma forms a volcano, cools, and hardens. Their are over 700 types of igneous rocks. Granite, basalt, and pumice is examples of igneous rocks. The upper part of Earth's crust is mostly made of igneous rocks.

21. Underline the **two** sentences in the passage that contain mistakes in punctuation and grammar usage.

Directions: For Question 22, remember the rules of punctuation, and then answer the question.

22. Choose the sentence that is punctuated correctly.

- ○ A. "I went to the information desk," and said please help me find books about penguins.
- ○ B. I went to the information desk and said, "that I needed someone to help me find books about penguins."
- ○ C. "I went to the information desk and said, Please help me find books about penguins."
- ○ D. I went to the information desk and said, "Please help me find books about penguins."

Directions: For Question 23, a student made a plan for a research report. Read the plan and the directions that follow.

Research Report Plan

Topic: Colonial Times

Audience: students in social studies class

Purpose: to inform

Research Question: What was daily life like for colonists during early Colonial Times?

---

23. The student found a source for the research report. Read the source below. Underline **one** sentence that has information that answers the research question.

America began as colonies that were located along the east coast from what is now Maine to Georgia. Colonies are groups of people who have left their native country to form in settlements in a new land. Settlers from Spain, France, Sweden, Holland, and England started American colonies starting in the 17th century. The settlers were called colonists. It was very challenging to start colonies in a new, unsettled land. The men and women had to build homes using just trees for materials and figure out how to provide themselves with food to keep from going hungry. Even though life was hard, more and more people came to the New World.

Performance Task

Student Directions:

And the Winner Is . . . Opinion Performance Task

Task

Your school's history club has prepared *museum displays* featuring Americans who have had an impact on American life. Each display includes an explanation of the person's accomplishments. The school newspaper has asked you to visit the museum, read the explanations, and write an opinion essay briefly describing three of the Americans and your top choice for who has impacted American life the most.

After you have looked at these sources, you will answer some questions about them. Briefly scan the sources and the three questions that follow. Then, go back and read the sources carefully so that you will have the information you will need to answer the questions and support your opinion essay. You may click on the Global Notes button to take notes on the information you find in the sources as you read. You may also use scratch paper to take notes.

In Part 2, you will write an opinion essay using information you have read.

Directions for Beginning:

You will now look at three sources. You can look at any of the sources as often as you like.

Research Questions:

After reviewing the research sources, use the rest of the time in Part 1 to answer three questions. Your answers to these questions will be scored. Also, your answers will help you think about the information you have read, which should help you write your opinion essay.

You may click on the Global Notes button or refer back to your scratch paper to review your notes when you think it would be helpful. Answer the questions in the spaces below the items.

Both the Global Notes on the computer and your written notes on scratch paper will be available to you in Part 1 and Part 2 of the Performance Task.

Part 1

Source #1

Read the museum display's explanation about Milton Hershey.

Hershey: More Than Just Chocolate
presented by Charnan Simon

One man who knew all about trying and failing was Milton Snavely Hershey. He tried to set up his own business many times. Each time he failed miserably. He lost all of his own money and the money of his friends and family. But Milton was stubborn. He knew he had a good idea, and he was determined to make it work.

Today, we can all be grateful for Milton Hershey's stubbornness. His good idea was the Hershey Chocolate Company. Thanks to Milton's hard work and determination, we have Hershey's candy bars, chocolate syrup, cocoa, and other treats to sweeten our world.

Milton Hershey made a lot of money from his chocolate company. He wanted to use his money in a worthwhile way. Instead of spending it all on himself, he used his money to help other people.

Milton Hershey built an entire town called Hershey, Pennsylvania. In this town he built homes, schools, and churches. He also built theaters, swimming pools, a sports arena, and an amusement park.

Perhaps more importantly, Milton Hershey started a school for disadvantaged children. Milton knew what it was like to be young and penniless. He had no children of his own, but that didn't stop him from wanting to help other children. He gave his entire personal fortune to the school that is named after him. Today, the Milton Hershey School serves more than one thousand boys and girls.

Source #2

Read the museum display's explanation about Sally Ride.

Sally Ride
presented by Joel Ayrton

Sally Ride was an inspiration to women and kids all over the world. She is officially the first American woman who travelled to space.

Early Life

Sally Kristen Ride was born on May 26, 1951, in Encino, California. Growing up she was a bright student who loved science and math. She also was an athlete and enjoyed playing tennis. She became one of the top ranked tennis players in the country.

After high school, she went to Stanford University in California. She earned degrees in physics. Physics is a type of science.

Becoming an Astronaut

In 1977, Sally saw an ad in the college's newspaper about NASA looking for astronauts. Over 8,000 people applied, but only 25 people were hired. Sally was one of six women picked!

First Woman in Space

On June 18, 1983, Sally Ride made history as the first American woman in space. She was an astronaut on the 7th space shuttle mission. She was 32 years old. Her job was to work the robotic arm. She used the arm to help put satellites into space. Sally said it was the most fun she had ever had.

Sally flew on the space shuttle again in 1984 on the 13th shuttle mission. She became the first woman to return to space.

Both missions were a success. They deployed satellites, ran scientific experiments, and helped NASA to continue to learn more about space and space flight.

Later Work

When Sally stopped working for NASA in 1987, she taught college classes. She also started her own company called Sally Ride Science, whose goal was to motivate more students to study science and math.

In 2003, Sally Ride was added to the Astronaut Hall of Fame. The Astronaut Hall of Fame honors astronauts for their hard work.

Until her death on July 23, 2012, Sally Ride continued to help students—especially girls—study science and mathematics. She wrote science books for children including *Mission Planet Earth* and *Exploring our Solar System*. She worked with science programs and festivals around the United States. She was a champion for science education and a role model for generations.

Source #3

Read the museum display's explanation about Benjamin Franklin.

The First American
presented by Kristen Bartlett

Benjamin Franklin is considered one of the greatest Americans that ever lived. He was a man of many talents and excelled in many areas including science, inventing, politics, writing, music, and diplomacy. He is one of the founding fathers of the United States of America and is often called the "First American."

Benjamin Franklin created many systems that changed the lives of Americans not only in his lifetime, but for Americans for centuries to come. His work from 300 years ago changed the way we live and work today.

The following timeline shows a few of his important accomplishments:

1700	
1710	
1720	
1730	**1731—Public Libraries:** In the early 18th century, books were mainly available to wealthy people. In 1731, Franklin developed the system that is the model for today's pubic libraries.
	1736—Fire Department: In 1736, Franklin organized the first volunteer fire department in Philadelphia. The success led to other volunteer fire departments in the city.
	1737—Post Office: Franklin became Philadelphia's postmaster in 1737. During his lifetime, he helped create regular mail routes, a standard price structure, and a system for inspecting mail service. Many of his systems are still in use by the postal service today.
1740	
1750	**1751—Public Hospitals:** Franklin was one of the founders of the Pennsylvania Hospital in 1751, which was the first public hospital in the country. Before this, there was no public health system for the poor. The public hospital system that Americans know today is modeled after the Pennsylvania Hospital.
1760	
1770	**1776—Declaration of Independence:** Franklin was one of 5 leaders chosen to write a document explaining why the 13 American Colonies wanted their freedom from England. The Declaration of Independence was adopted on July 4, 1776.
1780	

Research Questions

1. Source #1 discusses how Milton Hershey helped children by building a school. Explain how the information in Source #2 adds to the reader's understanding of how people have helped children learn. Give **two** details from Source #2 to support your explanation. Write your answer in the space below.

---

2. The following question has two parts. First answer Part A. Then answer Part B.

Part A: Which source would *most likely* be the most helpful in understanding who impacted the most Americans?

O A. Source #1
O B. Source #2
O C. Source #3

Part B: Explain why the source you selected in Part A is *most likely* the most helpful.

Use **two** details from the source to support your explanation. Write your answer in the space below.

----

3. Put a check mark in the boxes to match each source with the idea or ideas that it supports. Some ideas may have more than one source selected.

	Source #1: Hershey: More Than Just Chocolate	Source #2: Sally Ride	Source #3: The First American
Helping poor people is one way to be a good American.	☐	☐	☐
Being the first person to accomplish something can be inspirational to people.	☐	☐	☐
Using your personal wealth to help others can have a big impact on American life.	☐	☐	☐

On the actual test, you will click on the boxes to make your selections.

Directions for Part 2

You will now review your notes and sources, and plan, draft, revise, and edit your writing. You may use your notes and go back to the sources. Now read your assignment and the information about how your writing will be scored, and then begin your work.

Your Assignment

Your school's newspaper wants you to write an opinion essay briefly describing three of the Americans from the history club's museum display and your top choice for who has impacted American life the most. Your essay will be read by other students, teachers, and parents.

Using more than one source, choose the most important information to develop your opinion about which American impacted American life the most. Make sure to include reasons for your opinion as well as support for your reasons from the sources using your own words. Be sure to develop your opinion clearly.

Remember, a well-written opinion essay:

- ✔ explains your opinion clearly.
- ✔ is well organized and stays on topic.
- ✔ provides evidence from the sources to support your opinion.
- ✔ uses clear language.
- ✔ follows the rules of writing (spelling, punctuation, and grammar).

HOW YOUR ESSAY WILL BE SCORED

The people scoring your essay will be assigning scores for

1. **Statement of Purpose/Focus**—how well you clearly state your opinions on the topic and maintain your focus
2. **Organization**—how well your ideas logically flow from the introduction to the conclusion using effective transitions and how well you stay on topic throughout the essay
3. **Elaboration of Narrative**—how well you provide evidence from sources about your opinions and elaborate with specific information
4. **Language and Vocabulary**—how well you effectively express ideas using precise language that is appropriate for your purpose
5. **Conventions**—how well you follow the rules or usage, punctuation, capitalization, and spelling

Now begin work on your opinion essay. Manage your time carefully so that you can

1. Plan your essay.
2. Write your essay.
3. Revise and edit the final draft of your essay.

On the actual test, word-processing tools and a spell checker will be available to you. Also, on the actual test, since you will be writing an opinion essay that is several paragraphs long, you will type your response in a box that will get bigger as you type.

Remember to check your notes and your prewriting/planning as you write and then revise and edit your opinion essay.

English Language Arts Answers Explained

Computer-Adaptive Test, page 59

1. **(D)** To help figure out this answer, you needed to look for clues in the words surrounding "stern." The sentence says "stern and serious." When people are stern, they are not smiling. Choices B and C are not the most likely meanings of "stern." A stern person *may* be angry or mean, but not always. Choice A does not make sense with the rest of the sentence.

   Scoring Rubric: 1 point if the correct response is selected.

2. **(B)** Unlike the other animals, who could not agree about daylight and darkness, the chipmunk was certain that daylight would come.

   Scoring Rubric: 1 point if the correct response is selected.

3. **Part A: (B)** The porcupine called all the animals together to help them make a decision about daylight or darkness. He did not make the decision on his own nor did he let one of the animals make the decision for everyone. This should make you think (infer) that the porcupine was a fair leader.

   Part B: (D) This quote from the text is the only answer choice that supports the answer in Part A.

   Scoring Rubric: 1 point if the correct responses are selected for *both* Part A and Part B.

4. Answers will vary. Below is a sample response.

   Chipmunks have stripes on their backs because, long ago, a bear was angry that there would not be darkness all the time. When the chipmunk squeaked, "What did I tell you?" the bear chased the chipmunk. Just as the chipmunk reached its hole in a hollow tree, the bear struck him with his paw. His claws made black stripes on the chipmunk's back.

Scoring Rubric:

3 points	A response that
	• gives sufficient evidence of the ability to identify or summarize central ideas, key events, or procedures; • includes explanations that make reference to the text; and • fully supports the explanations with clearly relevant information from the text.
2 points	A response that
	• gives some evidence of the ability to identify or summarize central ideas, key events, or procedures; • includes some specific explanations that make reference to the text; and • adequately supports the explanations with relevant details and information from the text.
1 point	A response that
	• gives limited evidence of the ability to identify or summarize central ideas, key events, or procedures; • includes explanations, but they are not explicit or make only vague reference to the text; and • supports the explanations with at least one detail, but the relevance of that detail to the text must be inferred.
0 points	A response that
	• gives no evidence of the ability to use, identify, or summarize central ideas, key events, or procedures and includes no relevant information from the text.

Rubric from *http://www.rcoe.us/educational-services/files/2013/11/asmt-sbac-ela-gr4-sample-items.pdf*

5. **(B)** Choices A, C, and D do not make sense based on the details in the passage.

Scoring Rubric: 1 point if the correct response is selected.

6. **(B)** Choice B is correct because the details that the author uses about spiders and insects in the first paragraph explain the differences between the two creatures. Choices A and D are only details the author includes in the paragraph. They do not represent the author's purpose for that paragraph. Choice C suggests that the author is trying to convince the reader of something, but in the first paragraph, the author is explaining, not persuading.

Scoring Rubric: 1 point if the correct response is selected.

7. **(A)** "Biting" is a synonym for "piercing." The sentence in this question is from the first paragraph in the passage, which explains the differences between spiders and insects. It says that insects have jaws that "chew," so spiders have jaws that do not chew. The action of biting can be considered the opposite of chewing. Choices B and C are not the opposite of chewing. Choice D is an action that is the same as chewing.

Scoring Rubric: 1 point if the correct response is selected.

8. **(B), (D)**, and **(E)** The other details may be interesting, but they are not **key** details about spiders from the passage.

Scoring Rubric: 1 point if all three correct responses are selected.

9. Answers will vary. Below is a sample response.

> The lesson learned from this story is that little by little does the trick. The crow's work was slow, but he was patient and kept filling the pitcher with pebbles one at a time. In the end, his persistence paid off when he took a good long drink of water.

The sample response above describes an inference that can be made about what lesson the reader can learn from the crow. It follows the R.A.C.E. strategy framework: **R**estate the question to start your answer, **A**nswer the question, **C**ite evidence from the text, **E**xplain the reasoning for your answer.

Scoring Rubric:

3 points	A response that • gives sufficient evidence of the ability to use implicit information from the text to support an inference; • includes specific information and details that make reference to the text; and • fully supports the inference with clearly relevant information from the text.
2 points	A response that • gives some evidence of the ability to use implicit information from the text to support an inference; • includes some specific details that are information and details that make reference to the text; and • adequately supports the inferences with relevant details and information from the text.
1 point	A response that • gives limited evidence of the ability to use implicit information from the text to support an inference; • includes information that is not explicit or makes only vague reference to the text; and • supports the inference with at least one detail, but the relevance of that detail to the text must be inferred.
0 points	A response that • gives no evidence of the ability to use implicit information from the text to support an inference, includes no relevant information from the text, or is vague.

Rubric from *http://www.rcoe.us/educational-services/files/2013/11/asmt-sbac-ela-gr4-sample-items.pdf*

10. Answers will vary. Below is a sample response.

The author of the poem does not like going to bed in the summer because it is still daylight at his bedtime. He can hear the birds and the people who are still awake. He wishes he could play while it is light out instead of going to bed.

This response describes an inference that can be made about why the author of the poem does not like going to bed in the summer. It follows the R.A.C.E. strategy framework: **R**estate the question to start your answer, **A**nswer the question, **C**ite evidence from the text, **E**xplain the reasoning for your answer.

Scoring Rubric:

3 points	A response that
	• gives sufficient evidence of the ability to use implicit information from the text to support an inference;
	• includes specific information and details that make reference to the text; and
	• fully supports the inference with clearly relevant information from the text.
2 points	A response that
	• gives some evidence of the ability to use implicit information from the text to support an inference;
	• includes some specific details that are information and details that make reference to the text; and
	• adequately supports the inferences with relevant details and information from the text.
1 point	A response that
	• gives limited evidence of the ability to use implicit information from the text to support an inference;
	• includes information that is not explicit or makes only vague reference to the text; and
	• supports the inference with at least one detail, but the relevance of that detail to the text must be inferred.
0 points	A response that
	• gives no evidence of the ability to use implicit information from the text to support an inference, includes no relevant information from the text, or is vague.

Rubric from *http://www.rcoe.us/educational-services/files/2013/11/asmt-sbac-ela-gr4-sample-items.pdf*

11. **Part A: (B)** Choice B is correct because the details in the passage tell you that the narrator became an astronaut so that she could travel in space, but she did not realize how much hard work there would be.

    Part B: (B) This quote from the text is the only answer choice that supports the answer in Part A.

    Scoring Rubric: 1 point if the correct responses are selected for *both* Part A and Part B.

12. **(B)** To help figure out this answer, you needed to look for clues in the words surrounding "fatigued." The sentence in this question says that the narrator has already been awake for 20 hours and that it is her duty to stay awake. This helps you realize that "fatigued" most likely means "tired." Choice A might make sense, but it is not the most likely meaning based on the details in the sentence. Choices C and D do not make sense with details in the sentence.

    Scoring Rubric: 1 point if the correct response is selected.

13. Answers will vary. Below is a sample response.

    Gabby Douglas is a gymnast who wanted to do gymnastics from a young age and went on to win gold medals at the Olympics. She started taking gymnastics lessons when she was 6 years old and won her first championship when she was 8 years old. She went on to win a gold medal at the 2012 Olympics when she was 16 years old. She was nicknamed the "Flying Squirrel" because she did high-flying tricks on the uneven bars.

    The sample response above describes a summary that can be written using ideas and key details about Gabby Douglas from the passage.

Scoring Rubric:

3 points	A response that
	• gives sufficient evidence of the ability to identify or summarize central ideas, key events, or procedures; • includes explanations that make reference to the text; and • fully supports the explanations with clearly relevant information from the text.
2 points	A response that
	• gives some evidence of the ability to identify or summarize central ideas, key events, or procedures; • includes some specific explanations that make reference to the text; and • adequately supports the explanations with relevant details and information from the text.
1 point	A response that
	• gives limited evidence of the ability to identify or summarize central ideas, key events, or procedures; • includes explanations, but they are not explicit or make only vague reference to the text; and • supports the explanations with at least one detail, but the relevance of that detail to the text must be inferred.
0 points	A response that
	• gives no evidence of the ability to use, identify, or summarize central ideas, key events, or procedures and includes no relevant information from the text.

Rubric from *http://www.rcoe.us/educational-services/files/2013/11/asmt-sbac-ela-gr4-sample-items.pdf*

14. **(D)** Choice D is the best detail to use to revise the paragraph because it includes a descriptive verb, and the adjective "arched" describes the stripes of color. Choices A, B, and C make sense as replacements for the underlined phrase, but they are not precise descriptions.

Scoring Rubric: 1 point if the correct response is selected.

15. **(B)** "Burst" is a synonym for "break" and best describes the action of the bubble. Choice C makes sense as a replacement for the underlined word, but it is not the best description of the action of the bubble. Choices A and D do not make sense in the sentence.

    Scoring Rubric: 1 point if the correct response is selected.

16. **(C)** Choice C is the correct way to use an apostrophe to show that the noses belong to more than one dog.

    Scoring Rubric: 1 point if the correct response is selected.

17. Answers will vary. Below is a sample response.

    The author's most likely purpose for writing about Thomas Edison as a child and a young man is to tell the reader that Edison's interest in science and inventions started when he was a boy. In paragraph 2, the author wrote, "Young Edison set up a chemical laboratory in the cellar of their large house, where he liked to make experiments." As a young man, he worked hard and took things apart to see how they worked. In paragraph 4, the author wrote, "In his 20s, Edison moved to New York City, where he invented and patented his first invention, the electric vote recorder." That experiment was a failure, but he stuck to it and went on to invent 1,093 inventions! Edison's interest in science as a young boy most likely was the reason he went on to become a famous inventor.

    The sample response above describes an inference about the author's *most likely* purpose for writing about Thomas Edison as a child and a young man. It follows the R.A.C.E. strategy framework: **R**estate the question to start your answer, **A**nswer the question, **C**ite evidence from the text, **E**xplain the reasoning for your answer. One way that this response cites evidence is by using quotations from the text.

Scoring Rubric:

3 points	A response that
	• gives sufficient evidence of the ability to explain the author's most likely purpose for writing about Thomas Edison as a child and a young man;
	• includes specific examples that make clear reference to the text; and
	• fully supports the inferences with clearly relevant information from the text.
2 points	A response that
	• gives some evidence of the ability to explain the author's most likely purpose for writing about Thomas Edison as a child and a young man;
	• includes some specific examples that make reference to the text; and
	• adequately supports the inferences with relevant details and information from the text.
1 point	A response that
	• gives limited evidence of the ability to explain the author's most likely purpose for writing about Thomas Edison as a child and a young man;
	• includes examples, but they are not explicit or make only vague reference to the text; and
	• supports the inferences with at least one example, but the relevance of that example to the text must be inferred.
0 points	A response that
	• gives no evidence of the ability to explain the author's most likely purpose for writing about Thomas Edison as a child and a young man and includes no relevant information from the text.

Rubric from *http://www.rcoe.us/educational-services/files/2013/11/asmt-sbac-ela-gr4-sample-items.pdf*

18. Answers will vary. Below is a sample response.

> Our class took a trip to an exciting place with animals—the zoo. At the zoo, we learned about animals and had fun at the same time. We went to many different animal exhibits.

This sample introduction states the main idea of the zoo report and sets up what will follow in the body of the report, showing that the zoo is an exciting place.

Scoring Rubric:

2 points	The response
	• introduces an adequate statement of the main idea/ controlling idea that reflects the stimulus as a whole; • provides adequate information to put the main idea/ controlling idea into context; • does more than list points/reasons to support the main idea /controlling idea; and • connects smoothly to the body paragraphs.
1 point	The response
	• provides a partial or limited introduction of the main idea/controlling idea that partially reflects or just restates the stimulus; • may provide general and/or extraneous information to put the main idea/controlling idea into context; • may list supporting points and reasons for the main idea /controlling idea; and • provides a limited and/or awkward connection to the body paragraphs.
0 points	The response
	• provides no introduction or an inadequate or inappropriate main idea/controlling idea based on the stimulus; • provides irrelevant or no information to put the main idea/controlling idea into context; and • provides no connection to the body paragraphs.

19. **(C)** and **(F)** These two sentences *best* support the underlined opinion in the passage. The other sentences do not best support the opinion in the passage or do not connect to the opinion at all.

    Scoring Rubric: 1 point if the two correct responses are selected.

20. **(C)** Choice C is the best choice because it most clearly describes that the woman needed help when she fell out of her canoe without a life jacket. The word "begging" implies that she needs help immediately. Choices A, B, and D could fill in the blank, but they do not best describe the high importance of this event.

    Scoring Rubric: 1 point if the correct response is selected.

21. The two sentences that you should have underlined are **"Their are over 700 types of igneous rocks."** and **"Granite, basalt, and pumice is examples of igneous rocks."** In the first of these sentences, "Their" should be spelled "There." In the second of these sentences, there is incorrect grammar usage. Correct grammar usage would use "are" instead of "is" when referring to the plural "examples."

    Scoring Rubric: 1 point if the correct responses are selected.

22. **(D)** Choice D is the only sentence that is punctuated correctly, using the proper placement for commas, periods, and quotation marks.

    Scoring Rubric: 1 point if the correct response is selected.

23. You should have underlined the following sentence: **"The men and women had to build homes using just trees for materials and figure out how to provide themselves with food to keep from going hungry."** This is the sentence that answers the research question by explaining what daily life was like for colonists during early Colonial times.

    Scoring Rubric: 1 point if the correct response is selected.

Performance Task, page 78

Part 1

1. Answers will vary. Below is a sample response.

> Source #2, Sally Ride, adds to the reader's understanding of how people have helped children. The author explained that Sally Ride started a company "whose goal was to motivate more students to study science and math." Another detail from Source #2 is that Sally Ride wrote science books for children. This helped children learn about space.

The sample response above describes two details from Source #2 that add to the reader's understanding of how these people have helped children.

Scoring Rubric:

2 points	The response • is an evidence-based explanation that provides two pieces of evidence from the specified source that support this idea and that explain how each detail supports the idea.
1 point	The response • is an evidence-based explanation that provides two pieces of evidence from the specified source that support this idea but doesn't explain how each detail supports the idea. or • is an evidence-based explanation that provides only one piece of evidence from the specified source that supports this idea and that explains how that detail supports the idea.
0 points	The response • is an explanation that is incorrect, irrelevant, insufficient, or blank.

2. **Part A: (C)** Source #3 is *most likely* the most helpful in understanding who impacted the most Americans.

   Part B: Answers will vary. Below is a sample response.

   Source #3, The First American, has a timeline that includes details about some of Benjamin Franklin's accomplishments. One detail from the timeline is that Benjamin Franklin's work on the Declaration of Independence helped to develop our country. All Americans benefit from his work. A second detail is that Benjamin Franklin developed the system that supports today's public libraries. Many, many people use public libraries.

   This sample response above describes two details from Source #3 that add to the reader's understanding of who impacted the most Americans. Other details include:

   - Benjamin Franklin developed the system that supports today's postal system. The postal system is a part of most Americans' daily lives.
   - Benjamin Franklin organized a volunteer fire department. To this day, volunteer fire departments help many people in need.
   - Benjamin Franklin was one of the founders of the first public hospitals. Public hospitals serve many Americans.

Scoring Rubric:

2 points	The response • is an evidence-based explanation that correctly identifies the most helpful source AND includes, from that source, two details that support this evaluation and that explain why each detail supports the idea that it is the most helpful source.
1 point	The response • is an evidence-based explanation that correctly identifies the most helpful source AND includes one detail from that source that supports this evaluation and that explains why each detail supports the idea that it is the most helpful source. or • is an evidence-based explanation that correctly identifies the most helpful source AND includes two details from that source that support this evaluation, but does not explain why each detail supports the idea that it is the most helpful source. or • is an evidence-based explanation that does not identify a source or does not correctly identify the most helpful source, but does include two details from the correct source and explains why each detail supports the idea that it is the most helpful source.
0 points	The response • is an explanation that is incorrect, irrelevant, insufficient, or blank.

3. Your completed chart should read as follows:

	Source #1: Hershey: More Than Just Chocolate	Source #2: Sally Ride	Source #3: The First American
Helping poor people is one way to be a good American.	☑	☐	☑
Being the first person to accomplish something can be inspirational to people.	☐	☑	☑
Using your personal wealth to help others can have a big impact on American life.	☑	☐	☐

These answer choices are supported by information from the three sources.

Scoring Rubric: 1 point if all 5 correct cells are marked. 0 points if fewer than the 5 correct cells are marked.

Part 2

Answers will vary. Below is a sample response.

And the Winner Is . . .

by Kelly Kane

The history club recently prepared museum displays featuring Americans who have had an impact on American life. Three of the Americans in the museum were Milton Hershey, Sally Ride, and Benjamin Franklin.

Milton Hershey has had an impact on American life because he built an entire town with the money he made from his chocolate company. According to the Milton Hershey display, "He wanted to use his money in a worthwhile way. Instead of spending it all on himself, he used his money to help other people." In particular, he built a school for disadvantaged children. The display states that "Today, the Milton Hershey School serves more than one thousand boys and girls."

Sally Ride has had an impact on American life because she was the first American woman in space. She went into space twice. According to the Sally Ride display, "Both missions were a success. They deployed satellites, ran scientific experiments, and helped NASA to continue to learn more about space and space flight." She started her own company whose goal was to motivate more students to study science and math. The display also notes that "She was a champion for science education and a role model for generations."

Benjamin Franklin has had an impact on American life because he "created many systems that changed the lives of Americans not only in his lifetime, but for Americans for centuries to come." His accomplishments include creating the first public library, developing the post office, organizing the first volunteer fire department in Philadelphia, and helping to start the first American public hospital. As the Benjamin Franklin display states, "He was a man of many talents."

Based on what I read, my opinion of the top choice for the person who has impacted American life the most is Benjamin Franklin. Not only did he create things that help many people, but he was also one of the founding fathers of our country. He was one of the authors of the Declaration of Independence, which gave Americans freedom. Additionally, he is called the First American. Most importantly, "His work from 300 years ago changed the way we live and work today." Thank you, Benjamin Franklin!

Writing details that help make this essay effective include:

1. **Statement of Purpose/Focus**—how well you clearly state your opinions on the topic and maintain your focus.

   - This sample essay maintains focus by sticking to the descriptions of the people from the museum displays.
   - The opinion for the top choice for the person who has impacted American life the most is clearly stated.

2. **Organization**—how well your ideas logically flow from the introduction to the conclusion using effective transitions and how well you stay on topic throughout the essay.

   - The sample essay is organized into paragraphs. Each paragraph has a specific topic.
   - The ideas logically flow from introducing the museum displays to describing the impact each of the three people had on American life, and finally ending with an opinion of which person had the most impact.
   - Linking words and phrases, such as "in particular," "additionally," and "most importantly," are used.

3. **Elaboration of Narrative**—how well you provide evidence from sources about your opinions and elaborate with specific information.

   - This sample essay includes seven pieces of textual evidence (information from the text) to support the essay's ideas.
   - When the exact words an author wrote were used in the essay, quotation marks were around those words to help the reader know that they were the author's words.

4. **Language and Vocabulary**—how well you effectively express ideas using precise language that is appropriate for your purpose.

- This sample essay uses precise language ("role model," "accomplishments") that is appropriate for the purpose.

5. **Conventions**—how well you follow the rules or usage, punctuation, capitalization, and spelling.

- All usage, punctuation, capitalization, and spelling are correct in this essay.

Below are the Smarter Balanced official scoring rubrics for an Opinion Essay.

4-Point
Opinion
Performance Task Writing Rubric (Grades 3–5)

Score	
4	**PURPOSE/ORGANIZATION** **The response has a clear and effective organizational structure, creating a sense of unity and completeness. The response is fully sustained and consistently and purposefully focused:** • opinion is introduced, clearly communicated, and the focus is strongly maintained for the purpose, audience, and task • consistent use of a variety of transitional strategies to clarify the relationships between and among ideas • effective introduction and conclusion • logical progression of ideas from beginning to end; strong connections between and among ideas with some syntactic variety **EVIDENCE/ELABORATION** **The response provides thorough and convincing support/evidence for the opinion and supporting idea(s) that includes the effective use of sources, facts, and details. The response clearly and effectively expresses ideas, using precise language:** • comprehensive evidence from sources is integrated; references are relevant and specific • effective use of a variety of elaborative techniques* • vocabulary is clearly appropriate for the audience and purpose • effective, appropriate style enhances content

Score	
3	**PURPOSE/ORGANIZATION** **The response has an evident organizational structure and a sense of completeness, though there may be minor flaws and some ideas may be loosely connected. The response is adequately sustained and generally focused:** • opinion is clear, and the focus is mostly maintained for the purpose, audience, and task • adequate use of transitional strategies with some variety to clarify relationships between and among ideas • adequate introduction and conclusion • adequate progression of ideas from beginning to end; adequate connections between and among ideas **EVIDENCE/ELABORATION** **The response provides adequate support/evidence for the opinion and supporting idea(s) that includes the use of sources, facts, and details. The response adequately expresses ideas, employing a mix of precise with more general language:** • adequate evidence from sources is integrated; some references may be general • adequate use of some elaborative techniques • vocabulary is generally appropriate for the audience and purpose • generally appropriate style is evident
2	**PURPOSE/ORGANIZATION** **The response has an inconsistent organizational structure, and flaws are evident. The response is somewhat sustained and may have a minor drift in focus:** • opinion may be somewhat unclear, or the focus may be insufficiently sustained for the purpose, audience, and task • inconsistent use of transitional strategies and/or little variety • introduction or conclusion, if present, may be weak • uneven progression of ideas from beginning to end; and/or formulaic; inconsistent or unclear connections between and among ideas

Score	
2 (Cont'd.)	**EVIDENCE/ELABORATION** **The response provides uneven, cursory support/evidence for the opinion and supporting idea(s) that includes partial or uneven use of sources, facts, and details. The response expresses ideas unevenly, using simplistic language:** • some evidence from sources may be weakly integrated, imprecise, or repetitive; references may be vague • weak or uneven use of elaborative techniques; development may consist primarily of source summary • vocabulary use is uneven or somewhat ineffective for the audience and purpose • inconsistent or weak attempt to create appropriate style **CONVENTIONS** **The response demonstrates an adequate command of conventions:** adequate use of correct sentence formation, punctuation, capitalization, grammar usage, and spelling
1	**PURPOSE/ORGANIZATION** **The response has little or no discernible organizational structure. The response may be related to the opinion but may provide little or no focus:** • opinion may be confusing or ambiguous; response may be too brief or the focus may drift from the purpose, audience, or task • few or no transitional strategies are evident • introduction and/or conclusion may be missing • frequent extraneous ideas may be evident; ideas may be randomly ordered or have an unclear progression

Score	
1 (Cont'd.)	**EVIDENCE/ELABORATION**
	The response provides minimal support/evidence for the opinion and supporting idea(s) that includes little or no use of sources, facts, and details. The response's expression of ideas is vague, lacks clarity, or is confusing:
	• evidence from the source material is minimal or irrelevant; references may be absent or incorrectly used
	• minimal, if any, use of elaborative techniques
	• vocabulary is limited or ineffective for the audience and purpose
	• little or no evidence of appropriate style
	CONVENTIONS
	The response demonstrates a partial command of conventions:
	• limited use of correct sentence formation, punctuation, capitalization, grammar usage, and spelling.
0	**CONVENTIONS**
	The response demonstrates little or no command of conventions:
	• infrequent use of correct sentence formation, punctuation, capitalization, grammar usage, and spelling
NS	**PURPOSE/ORGANIZATION**
	• Unintelligible • Off-topic
	• In a language other than English • Copied text
	• Off-purpose
	EVIDENCE/ELABORATION
	• Unintelligible • Off-topic
	• In a language other than English • Copied text
	• Off-purpose
	CONVENTIONS
	• Unintelligible • Off-topic
	• In a language other than English • Copied text
	(Off-purpose responses will still receive a score in Conventions.)

Rubrics from *http://www.smarterbalanced.org/wp-content/uploads/2015/09/Opinion_PT_Rubric.pdf*

Holistic Scoring:

- **Variety:** A range of errors includes formation, punctuation, capitalization, grammar usage, and spelling.
- **Severity:** Basic errors are more heavily weighted than higher-level errors.
- **Density:** The proportion of errors to the amount of writing done well. This includes the ratio of errors to the length of the piece.

While the Performance Task in this practice test focused on an Opinion Essay, it is also important for you to familiarize yourself with the expectations for the other two potential essay types on the Performance Task: the Narrative Essay and the Information Essay. First, take a look at the links below, which provide you with more practice examples for the ELA Performance Task. Then, read the scoring descriptions and official rubrics for each essay type.

Links and Information for More ELA Performance Task Practice

www.smarterbalanced.org/sample-items-and-performance-tasks

www.smarterbalanced.org/practice-test

www.ode.state.or.us/search/page/?id=3723

How a Narrative Essay Will Be Scored

This essay will be scored for:

1. **Narrative focus**—how well you maintain your focus and establish setting, the narrator, and/or the characters

2. **Organization**—how well the events logically flow from the beginning to the end using effective transitions and how well you stay on topic throughout the essay

3. **Elaboration of narrative**—how well you elaborate with details, dialogue, and descriptions to advance the story or illustrate the experience

4. **Language and vocabulary**—how well you effectively express experiences or events using sensory, concrete, and figurative language that is appropriate for your purpose

5. **Conventions**—how well you follow the rules of usage, punctuation, capitalization, and spelling

Below are the Smarter Balanced official scoring rubrics for a Narrative Essay.

4-Point
Narrative
Performance Task Writing Rubric (Grades 3–8)

Score	
4	**PURPOSE/ORGANIZATION** **The organization of the narrative, real or imagined, is fully sustained and the focus is clear and maintained throughout:** • an effective plot helps to create a sense of unity and completeness • effectively establishes and maintains setting, develops narrator/ characters, and maintains point of view • consistent use of a variety of transitional strategies to clarify the relationships between and among ideas; strong connection between and among ideas • natural, logical sequence of events from beginning to end • effective opening and closure for audience and purpose **DEVELOPMENT/ELABORATION** **The narrative, real or imagined, provides thorough, effective elaboration using relevant details, dialogue, and description:** • experiences, characters, setting and events are clearly developed • connections to source materials may enhance the narrative • effective use of a variety of narrative techniques that advance the story or illustrate the experience • effective use of sensory, concrete, and figurative language that clearly advances the purpose • effective, appropriate style enhances the narration

Score	
3	**PURPOSE/ORGANIZATION**
	The organization of the narrative, real or imagined, is adequately sustained, and the focus is adequate and generally maintained:
	• an evident plot helps to create a sense of unity and completeness, though there may be minor flaws and some ideas may be loosely connected
	• adequately maintains a setting, develops narrator/characters, and/or maintains point of view
	• adequate use of a variety of transitional strategies to clarify the relationships between and among ideas
	• adequate sequence of events from beginning to end
	• adequate opening and closure for audience and purpose
	DEVELOPMENT/ELABORATION
	The narrative, real or imagined, provides adequate elaboration using details, dialogue, and description:
	• experiences, characters, setting, and events are adequately developed
	• connections to source materials may contribute to the narrative
	• adequate use of a variety of narrative techniques that generally advance the story or illustrate the experience
	• adequate use of sensory, concrete, and figurative language that generally advances the purpose; generally appropriate style is evident
2	**PURPOSE/ORGANIZATION**
	The organization of the narrative, real or imagined, is somewhat sustained and may have an uneven focus:
	• there may be an inconsistent plot, and/or flaws may be evident
	• unevenly or minimally maintains a setting, develops narrator and/or characters, and/or maintains point of view
	• uneven use of appropriate transitional strategies and/or little variety
	• weak or uneven sequence of events
	• opening and closure, if present, are weak

Score	
2 (Cont'd.)	**DEVELOPMENT/ELABORATION** The narrative, real or imagined, provides uneven, cursory elaboration using partial and uneven details, dialogue, and description: • experiences, characters, setting, and events are unevenly developed • connections to source materials may be ineffective, awkward, or vague but do not interfere with the narrative • narrative techniques are uneven and inconsistent • partial or weak use of sensory, concrete, and figurative language that may not advance the purpose • inconsistent or weak attempt to create appropriate style **CONVENTIONS** The response demonstrates an adequate command of conventions: • adequate use of correct sentence formation, punctuation, capitalization, grammar usage, and spelling
1	**PURPOSE/ORGANIZATION** The organization of the narrative, real or imagined, may be maintained but may provide little or no focus: • there is little or no discernible plot or there may just be a series of events • may be brief or there is little to no attempt to establish a setting, narrator and/or characters, and/or point of view • few or no appropriate transitional strategies may be evident • little or no organization of an event sequence; frequent extraneous ideas and/or a major drift may be evident • opening and/or closure may be missing

Score	
1 **(Cont'd.)**	**DEVELOPMENT/ELABORATION** **The narrative, real or imagined, provides minimal elaboration using few or no details, dialogue, and/or description:** • experiences, characters, setting, and events may be vague, lack clarity, or confusing • connections to source materials, if evident, may detract from the narrative • use of narrative techniques may be minimal, absent, incorrect, or irrelevant • may have little or no use of sensory, concrete, or figurative language; language does not advance and may interfere with the purpose • little or no evidence of appropriate style **CONVENTIONS** **The response demonstrates a partial command of conventions:** • limited use of correct sentence formation, punctuation, capitalization, grammar usage, and spelling
0	**CONVENTIONS** **The response demonstrates little or no command of conventions:** • infrequent use of correct sentence formation, punctuation, capitalization, grammar usage, and spelling

NS	**PURPOSE/ORGANIZATION**
	
	• Unintelligible • Off-topic
	• In a language other • Copied text
	  than English • Off-purpose
	
	DEVELOPMENT/ELABORATION
	
	• Unintelligible • Off-topic
	• In a language other • Copied text
	  than English • Off-purpose
	
	CONVENTIONS
	
	• Unintelligible • Off-topic
	• In a language other • Copied text
	  than English
	
	(Off-purpose responses will still receive a score in Conventions.)

Rubrics from *http://www.smarterbalanced.org/wp-content/uploads/2015/09/Narrative_PT_Rubric.pdf*

Holistic Scoring:

- **Variety:** A range of errors includes formation, punctuation, capitalization, grammar usage, and spelling.
- **Severity:** Basic errors are more heavily weighted than higher-level errors.
- **Density:** The proportion of errors to the amount of writing done well. This includes the ratio of errors to the length of the piece.

How an Information Essay Will Be Scored

This essay will be scored for:

1. **Statement of Purpose/Focus**—how well you clearly state and maintain your controlling idea or main focus

2. **Organization**—how well the ideas progress from the introduction to the conclusion using effective transitions and how well you stay on topic throughout the essay

3. **Elaboration of narrative**—how well you provide evidence from the sources about your topic and elaborate with specific information

4. **Language and vocabulary**—how well you effectively express ideas using precise language that is appropriate for your purpose

5. **Conventions**—how well you follow the rules of usage, punctuation, capitalization, and spelling

Below are the Smarter Balanced official scoring rubrics for an Informational Essay.

4-Point
Informational
Performance Task Writing Rubric (Grades 3–5)

Score	
4	**PURPOSE/ORGANIZATION** **The response has a clear and effective organizational structure, creating a sense of unity and completeness. The response is fully sustained, and consistently and purposefully focused:** • controlling or main idea of a topic is clearly communicated, and the focus is strongly maintained for the purpose, audience, and task • consistent use of a variety of transitional strategies to clarify the relationships between and among ideas • effective introduction and conclusion • logical progression of ideas from beginning to end; strong connections between and among ideas with some syntactic variety **EVIDENCE/ELABORATION** **The response provides thorough and convincing support/evidence for the controlling idea and supporting idea(s) that includes the effective use of sources, facts, and details. The response clearly and effectively elaborates ideas, using precise language:** • comprehensive evidence from sources is integrated; references are relevant and specific • effective use of a variety of elaborative techniques* • vocabulary is clearly appropriate for the audience and purpose • effective, appropriate style enhances content

*Elaborative techniques may include the use of personal experiences that support the controlling idea.

Score	
3	**PURPOSE/ORGANIZATION** The response has an evident organizational structure and a sense of completeness, though there may be minor flaws and some ideas may be loosely connected. The response is adequately sustained and generally focused: • controlling or main idea of a topic is clear, and the focus is mostly maintained for the purpose, audience, and task • adequate use of transitional strategies with some variety to clarify the relationships between and among ideas • adequate introduction and conclusion • adequate progression of ideas from beginning to end; adequate connections between and among ideas **EVIDENCE/ELABORATION** The response provides adequate support/evidence for the controlling idea and supporting idea(s) that includes the use of sources, facts, and details. The response adequately elaborates ideas, employing a mix of precise and more general language: • adequate evidence from sources is integrated; some references may be general • adequate use of some elaborative techniques • vocabulary is generally appropriate for the audience and purpose • generally appropriate style is evident
2	**PURPOSE/ORGANIZATION** The response has an inconsistent organizational structure, and flaws are evident. The response is somewhat sustained and may have a minor drift in focus: • controlling or main idea of a topic may be somewhat unclear, or the focus may be insufficiently sustained for the purpose, audience, and task • inconsistent use of transitional strategies and/or little variety • introduction or conclusion, if present, may be weak • uneven progression of ideas from beginning to end; and/or formulaic; inconsistent or unclear connections between and among ideas

Score	
2 (Cont'd.)	**EVIDENCE/ELABORATION** **The response provides uneven, cursory support/evidence for the controlling idea and supporting idea(s) that includes uneven or limited use of sources, facts, and details. The response elaborates ideas unevenly, using simplistic language:** • some evidence from sources may be weakly integrated, imprecise, or repetitive; references may be vague • weak or uneven use of elaborative techniques; development may consist primarily of source summary • vocabulary use is uneven or somewhat ineffective for the audience and purpose • inconsistent or weak attempt to create appropriate style **CONVENTIONS** **The response demonstrates an adequate command of conventions:** • adequate use of correct sentence formation, punctuation, capitalization, grammar usage, and spelling
1	**PURPOSE/ORGANIZATION** **The response has little or no discernible organizational structure. The response may be related to the topic but may provide little or no focus:** • controlling or main idea may be confusing or ambiguous; response may be too brief or the focus may drift from the purpose, audience, or task • few or no transitional strategies are evident • introduction and/or conclusion may be missing • frequent extraneous ideas may be evident; ideas may be randomly ordered or have an unclear progression

Score	
1 **(Cont'd.)**	**EVIDENCE/ELABORATION** **The response provides minimal support/evidence for the controlling idea and supporting idea(s) that includes little or no use of sources, facts, and details. The response is vague, lacks clarity, or is confusing:** • evidence from the source material is minimal or irrelevant; references may be absent or incorrectly used • minimal, if any, use of elaborative techniques • vocabulary is limited or ineffective for the audience and purpose • little or no evidence of appropriate style **CONVENTIONS** **The response demonstrates a partial command of conventions:** • limited use of correct sentence formation, punctuation, capitalization, grammar usage, and spelling
0	**CONVENTIONS** **The response demonstrates little or no command of conventions:** • infrequent use of correct sentence formation, punctuation, capitalization, grammar usage, and spelling

NS	**PURPOSE/ORGANIZATION**
	
	 • Unintelligible • Off-topic
	 • In a language other • Copied text
	   than English • Off-purpose
	
	 DEVELOPMENT/ELABORATION
	
	 • Unintelligible • Off-topic
	 • In a language other • Copied text
	   than English • Off-purpose
	
	 CONVENTIONS
	
	 • Unintelligible • Off-topic
	 • In a language other • Copied text
	   than English
	
	 (Off-purpose responses will still receive a score in Conventions.)

Rubrics from http://www.smarterbalanced.org/wp-content/uploads/2015/09/Informational_PT_Rubric.pdf

Holistic Scoring:

- **Variety:** A range of errors includes formation, punctuation, capitalization, grammar usage, and spelling.
- **Severity:** Basic errors are more heavily weighted than higher-level errors.
- **Density:** The proportion of errors to the amount of writing done well. This includes the ratio of errors to the length of the piece.

PART TWO
Math

What Every Fourth Grader Needs to Know About Math

This chapter provides you with a summary of what "you," a fourth-grade student, will need to understand and be able to complete in your study of mathematics. You will be expected to show your understanding of the following key ideas and principles on the Smarter Balanced assessments. Your teacher will use the results of your tests to plan future lessons and help measure your progress. You and your parents should use your test results to understand your strengths and weaknesses and pinpoint skills that need to be developed further in order to be successful in your mathematical endeavors.

Three Instructional Critical Areas

The fourth-grade instructional focus, Common Core standards, and mathematical practices discussed in this chapter have been sourced from the official common core website (*www.corestandards.org*).

According to the Core Standards website:

In Grade 4, instructional time should focus on three critical areas: (1) developing understanding and fluency with multi-digit multiplication, and developing understanding of dividing to find quotients involving multi-digit dividends; (2) developing an understanding of fraction equivalence, addition and subtraction of fractions with like denominators, and multiplication of fractions by whole numbers; (3) understanding that geometric figures can be analyzed and classified based on their properties, such as having parallel sides, perpendicular sides, particular angle measures, and symmetry.

1. *Students generalize their understanding of place value to 1,000,000, understanding the relative sizes of numbers in each place. They apply their understanding of models for multiplication (equal-sized groups, arrays, and area models), place value, and properties of operations, in particular the distributive property, as they develop, discuss, and use efficient, accurate, and generalizable methods to compute products of multi-digit whole*

numbers. *Depending on the numbers and the context, they select and accurately apply appropriate methods to estimate or mentally calculate products. They develop fluency with efficient procedures for multiplying whole numbers; understand and explain why the procedures work based on place value and properties of operations; and use them to solve problems. Students apply their understanding of models for division, place value, properties of operations, and the relationship of division to multiplication as they develop, discuss, and use efficient, accurate, and generalizable procedures to find quotients involving multi-digit dividends. They select and accurately apply appropriate methods to estimate and mentally calculate quotients, and interpret remainders based upon the context.*

2. *Students develop understanding of fraction equivalence and operations with fractions. They recognize that two different fractions can be equal $\left(e.g., \dfrac{15}{9} = \dfrac{5}{3}\right)$, and they develop methods for generating and recognizing equivalent fractions. Students extend previous understandings about how fractions are built from unit fractions, composing fractions from unit fractions, decomposing fractions into unit fractions, and using the meaning of fractions and the meaning of multiplication to multiply a fraction by a whole number.*

3. *Students describe, analyze, compare, and classify two-dimensional shapes. Through building, drawing, and analyzing two-dimensional shapes, students deepen their understanding of properties of two-dimensional objects and the use of them to solve problems involving symmetry.*

Explanatory Materials/Methods and Key Vocabulary for Each Critical Area

To help better understand these three critical areas, review the following explanatory materials/methods and the key vocabulary that you will need to be familiar with for each area.

> Key vocabulary terms that you should be familiar with are in bold throughout this chapter. Make sure to study them carefully!

Critical Area 1

"Developing understanding and fluency with multi-digit multiplication, and developing understanding of dividing to find quotients involving multi-digit dividends."

Place value tells you how much each digit stands for. Our number system is based on a simple pattern of tens. Each place has ten times the value of the place to its right. Refer to Table 8-1 to better understand place value.

Table 8-1. Place Value

Thousands	Hundreds	Tens	Ones
1 thousand is 10 times 1 hundred	1 hundred is 10 times 1 ten	1 ten is 10 times 1	1 one is 1
10 × 100 = 1,000	10 × 10 = 100	10 × 1 = 10	1

We arrange numbers into groups of three places called **periods**. The places within periods repeat (hundreds, tens, ones; hundreds, tens, ones; and so on). In the United States, we typically use commas to separate the periods, but sometimes four-digit numbers are written without commas. For example, 2387 is the same as 2,387.

Example 1

What is the value of the digit **4** in 8,435,721?

In order to answer this question, create a table like the one below to see the value of each digit.

Millions Period			Thousands Period			Ones Period		
Hundreds	Tens	Ones	Hundreds	Tens	Ones	Hundreds	Tens	Ones
		8,	4	3	5,	7	2	1

As you can see from the table, the digit **4** is in the hundred thousands place. Its value is 4 hundred thousand, or 400,000.

Multiplication is the operation of repeated addition. For example, 3 × 4 is the same as 4 + 4 + 4 or 3 + 3 + 3 + 3. Two terms that are used in multiplication that you might come across are **factor** and **product**. Look at the following math problem:

$$9 \times 5 = 45$$

In this problem, the 9 is a factor, the 5 is another factor, and the 45 is the product.

If you know how to multiply 1-digit numbers, such as 6 × 7 = 42, then you can also multiply larger numbers, such as 6 × 777 = 4,662. You can determine this answer by multiplying only one digit at a time. Each product is called a partial product. Find all of the partial products, and then add them together to find the total product. In this case, the first partial product is 42 (which represents 6 × 7). The second partial product is 420 (which represents 6 × 70). The third partial product is 4,200 (which represents 6 × 700). When added altogether, 42 + 420 + 4,200 = 4,662.

Two common methods used in multiplying are **Partial-Products Multiplication** and **Traditional Multiplication**. Review Example 2 to see how both methods could be used to solve the problem.

Example 2

A gross equals 144. How many pencils are in 6 gross?

Using Partial-Products Multiplication

H	T	O	
1	4	4	
×		6	
	2	4	← *Multiply the Ones.* **6 × 4 ones = 6 × 4 = 24**
2	4	0	← *Multiply the Tens.* **6 × 4 tens = 6 × 40 = 240**
6	0	0	← *Multiply the Hundreds.* **6 × 1 hundred = 6 × 100 = 600**
8	6	4	← *Add the partial products.*

Using Traditional Multiplication

Step 1 ➡ **Step 2** ➡ **Step 3**

			H	T	O
Multiply the Ones	Multiply the Tens	Multiply the Hundreds			

6 × 4 ones = 24 ones   6 × 4 tens = 24 tens   6 × 1 hundred = 6 hundreds

	H	T	O
		2	2
	1	4	4
	×		6
	8	6	4

Write 4 in the ones place and write 2 above the tens so you don't forget about it.

Add the 4 tens to the 2 tens you already have. Write 6 in the tens place. Write 2 above the hundreds so you don't forget about it.

Add the 6 hundreds to the 2 hundreds you already have. Write 8 in the hundreds place.

In both methods, there are 864 pencils in a gross.

Arrays are an arrangement of objects in equal rows that model a multiplication equation. For example:

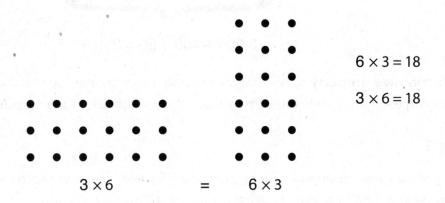

6 × 3 = 18

3 × 6 = 18

3 × 6   =   6 × 3

An **area model** is a picture representation of a multiplication or division problem. The model helps your visualize what is happening in the problem. For example:

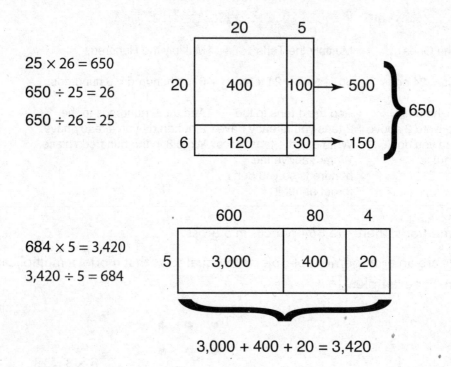

$$25 \times 26 = 650$$
$$650 \div 25 = 26$$
$$650 \div 26 = 25$$

$$684 \times 5 = 3{,}420$$
$$3{,}420 \div 5 = 684$$

$$3{,}000 + 400 + 20 = 3{,}420$$

The **distributive property** states that multiplying a sum by a number is the same as multiplying each number in the sum by that number and adding the products.

Example 3

The town of Sandown opened a new section of a bike trail. The new section is 6 yards wide and 1,842 yards long. What is the area of the new section?

Remember that area = length × width ($A = l \times w$). Therefore, 6 × 1,842 will give us the area of the new section of the bike trail.

Here is how you would use the distributive property to find 6 × 1,842:

$$6 \times 1{,}842 = 6 \times (1{,}000 + 800 + 40 + 2)$$
$$= (6 \times 1{,}000) + (6 \times 800) + (6 \times 40) + (6 \times 2)$$
$$= (6{,}000) + (4{,}800) + (240) + (12)$$
$$= 11{,}052$$

Therefore, the area of the new section of the bike trail is 11,052 square yards.

> As you can see, the distributive property can be used to break larger multiplication problems apart into several smaller problems that are easier to solve.

You can also **estimate**, which means finding a number that is close to the exact amount that you are looking for. An estimate tells you *about* how much or *about* how many.

Rounding is one way to estimate. When you round a number, you change it to a nearby number that will have "round" zeros at the end of it. There are two common methods used when rounding: using a number line and using place value. Example 4 shows how to use a number line, while Example 5 demonstrates using place value.

Example 4

Round 276 to the nearest hundred.

Rounding Numbers Using a Number Line:

200 is the closest hundred below 276. 300 is the closest hundred above 276. Look at where 276 falls on the number line below:

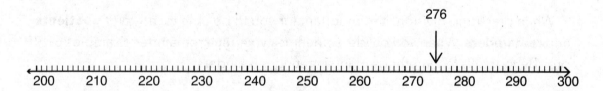

As you can see from the number line, 276 is closer to 300 than to 200. Therefore, 276 rounds up to 300.

Example 5

Round 362 to the nearest hundred.

Rounding Numbers Using Place Value:

First, find the hundreds place. In this case, 3 is in the hundreds place of 3̲62. Then, look at the digit one place to its right, which is 6 in this example. If that digit is 5 or more, round up. If the digit is less than 5, keep it the same, and make all the other digits to its right zeros. In this example, 6 is greater than 5 so we round up, meaning that, to the nearest hundred, 362 rounds up to 400.

Division creates equal groups. Terms that you may see used when talking about division are **dividend**, **divisor**, and **quotient**. Consider the following problem:

$$16 \div 2 = 8$$

Here, 16 is the dividend, 2 is the divisor, and 8 is the quotient. Or, think of it this way:

$$\text{divisor}\overline{)\text{dividend}}^{\text{quotient}}$$

Division and **multiplication** are opposites. Therefore, the fact that $6 \times 3 = 18$ and $3 \times 6 = 18$ is related to the fact that $18 \div 3 = 6$ and $18 \div 6 = 3$.

Below is one way to find a quotient:

$$4\overline{)25}$$

$$25 \div 4 = (6 \times 4 = 24) + 1$$

$$4\overline{)25}^{6R1}$$

When practicing division, it is important for you to be able to *interpret* **quotients** and **remainders**. When you divide, sometimes you get a remainder. Examples 6−9 provide four different methods of interpreting remainders.

Example 6

You have 21 ounces of M & Ms. How many 8-ounce bags can you fill?

Method 1: Ignore the Remainder.

$$
\begin{array}{r}
2R5 \\
8\overline{)21} \\
-16 \\
\hline
5
\end{array}
$$

The answer, 2R5, shows that you can fill 2 bags completely. The remainder, 5, tells you that there are 5 ounces of M & Ms not in a full bag. You do not need the remainder to answer this question. You only need to know how many 8-ounce bags you can *fill*. Since you cannot fill the third bag completely, you can ignore the remainder and answer that you can only fill <u>two</u> 8-ounce bags.

Example 7

On the flume ride at the amusement park, each boat holds 7 people. Seventy-five people are in line. How many boats will the ride operator need?

Method 2: The Answer Is the Next Whole Number.

$$
\begin{array}{r}
10\text{R}5 \\
7{\overline{\smash{)}}}\ 75 \\
-70 \\
\hline
5
\end{array}
$$

The answer, 10R5, shows that you cannot fit all of these people on 10 boats. You need one more boat to fit the other 5 people. Therefore, the answer must be the next whole number, which is 11. Therefore, the ride operator will need to gather 11 boats.

Example 8

You have 126 trading cards. You share the cards equally among 10 friends. You give them as many cards as you can. How many cards do you have left?

Method 3: Use the Remainder as the Answer.

$$
\begin{array}{r}
12\text{R}6 \\
10{\overline{\smash{)}}}\ 126 \\
-120 \\
\hline
6
\end{array}
$$

The remainder, 6, shows the number of cards that you have left. Therefore, you have 6 cards left over after you give your friends an equal share.

Example 9

Typists are needed to input a large book for a publisher. The entire job should take 38 hours. If 4 typists share the time to input the information equally, how long will each one work on the book?

Method 4: Write the Remainder as a Fraction.

$$\begin{array}{r} 9R2 \\ 4\overline{)\ 38} \\ -36 \\ \hline 2 \end{array}$$

The answer, 9R2, tells you that each typist will work 9 hours, and there will be an extra 2 hours that they all must share. To write the remainder as a fraction of time, write the remainder over the divisor.

$$\text{Remainder} \rightarrow \quad \frac{2}{4} \quad \leftarrow \text{Divisor}$$

Therefore, each typist will work $9\frac{2}{4}$ hours, which simplifies to $9\frac{1}{2}$ hours.

Critical Area 2

"Developing an understanding of fraction equivalence, addition and subtraction of fractions with like denominators, and multiplication of fractions by whole numbers."

A **fraction** is a symbol that stands for a part of something. The **numerator** (the number on top) represents your chosen parts. The **denominator** (the number on the bottom) represents how many equal parts there are in the whole set. The fraction $\frac{3}{4}$ represents 3 chosen parts of a group of 4.

Fractions can represent a part of one thing, a part of a set, a location on a number line, or a division of whole numbers. Examples 10–13 present examples of each of these fraction representations.

Example 10

Fraction Representation 1: Part of One Thing

$\frac{3}{8}$ = 3 of the 8 equal parts are shaded, as in the illustration below.

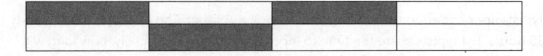

Example 11

Fraction Representation 2: Part of a Set

$\frac{2}{3}$ = 2 of the 3 hearts in the following set are shaded gray.

Example 12

Fraction Representation 3: A Location on a Number Line

$\frac{0}{4}$, $\frac{1}{4}$, $\frac{2}{4}$, $\frac{3}{4}$, and $\frac{4}{4}$ are all locations on the following number line.

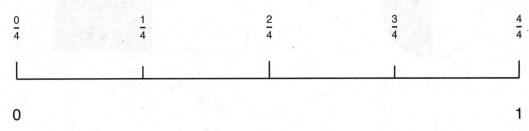

Example 13

Fraction Representation 4: A Division of Whole Numbers

$$\frac{12}{4} = 3$$

or

$$12 \div 4 = 3$$

or

The denominator, 4, goes into the numerator, 12, three times.

Equivalent fractions are two or more fractions that have the same value. For example:

$$\frac{1}{2} = \frac{2}{4} = \frac{4}{8} = \frac{5}{10} = \frac{12}{24}$$

To find equivalent fractions, you multiply or divide the numerator and the denominator by the same number. For example:

$$\frac{1}{2} = \frac{1 \times 4}{2 \times 4} = \frac{4}{8}$$

or

$$\frac{1}{2} = \frac{1 \times 5}{2 \times 5} = \frac{5}{10}$$

Equivalent fractions name the <u>same part</u> of the <u>same whole</u>. In other words, $\frac{1}{2}$ of a pizza is *not* the same as $\frac{1}{2}$ of a sandwich because they are not the same whole as shown below.

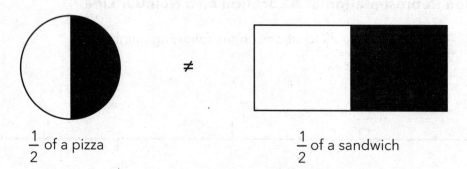

$\frac{1}{2}$ of a pizza $\frac{1}{2}$ of a sandwich

Sometimes, you might be asked to find a missing numerator or find a missing denominator in equivalent fractions. Examples 14 and 15 will help you understand this.

Example 14

$$\frac{5}{6} = \frac{?}{12}$$

To find the missing numerator (?), ask yourself, "What was the original denominator multiplied or divided by to get the new denominator?" When you find that answer, then do the same to the original numerator.

In this example, the original denominator, 6, was multiplied by 2 to get 12 as the new denominator. Therefore, the original numerator, 5, also needs to be multiplied by 2 to find the missing new numerator. $5 \times 2 = 10$. Therefore, the missing new numerator is 10.

$$\frac{5}{6} = \frac{10}{12}$$

Example 15

$$\frac{8}{12} = \frac{2}{?}$$

To find the missing denominator (?), ask yourself, "What was the original numerator multiplied or divided by to get the new numerator?" When you find that answer, then do the same to the original denominator.

In this example, the original numerator, 8, was divided by 4 to get the new numerator, 2. Therefore, the original denominator, 12, also needs to be divided by 4 to find the missing denominator. $12 \div 4 = 3$. Therefore, the new missing denominator is 3.

$$\frac{8}{12} = \frac{2}{3}$$

A **unit fraction** is a fraction with a numerator of 1. In other words, all units of a fraction have equal parts, like in the following illustration.

$$\frac{1}{6}$$

To **compose** means to separate into parts. You could compose $\frac{4}{5}$ as follows:

$$\frac{4}{5} = \frac{2}{5} + \frac{1}{5} + \frac{1}{5}$$

To **decompose** means to put parts together. You could decompose $\frac{3}{4}$ as follows:

$$\frac{3}{4} = \frac{1}{4} + \frac{1}{4} + \frac{1}{4}$$

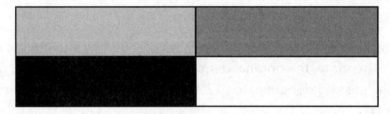

A **mixed number** is a number with a whole part and a fraction part. The mixed number $3\frac{3}{4}$ could be visually represented as:

$3\frac{3}{4} =$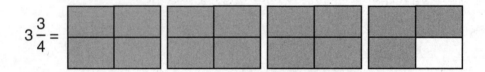

Adding and subtracting fractions with like denominators is another important skill for you to learn. To add or subtract fractions with like denominators, just add or subtract the numerators and keep the denominators the same.

Example 16

Adding Fractions with Like Denominators

$$\frac{2}{8} + \frac{3}{8} = \frac{5}{8}$$

Example 17

Subtracting Fractions with Like Denominators

$$\frac{10}{12} - \frac{4}{12} = \frac{6}{12}$$

Now that you know how to add and subtract fractions, how would you **multiply a fraction by a whole number**? There are three different methods of doing this: repeated addition, drawing a model, and multiplication. Each of these methods is demonstrated in Example 18.

Example 18

How much orange juice is needed so that 4 students can each get $\frac{1}{3}$ of a cup of juice?

Method 1: Repeated Addition

$$4 \times \frac{1}{3} = \frac{1}{3} + \frac{1}{3} + \frac{1}{3} + \frac{1}{3} = \frac{4}{3} = 1\frac{1}{3} \text{ cups are needed}$$

Method 2: Drawing a Model

4 students each get $\frac{1}{3}$ of a cup of juice

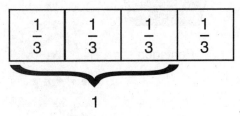

$1\frac{1}{3}$ cups are needed.

Method 3: Multiplication

$$4 \times \frac{1}{3} = \frac{4 \times 1}{3} = \frac{4}{3} = 1\frac{1}{3}$$

Critical Area 3

"Understanding that geometric figures can be analyzed and classified based on their properties, such as having parallel sides, perpendicular sides, particular angle measures, and symmetry."

Two-dimensional shapes are figures that are sometimes referred to as plane figures because they lie flat, in a single plane. They have the dimensions of length and width, making them two-dimensional. We can classify these figures as polygons, triangles, quadrilaterals, and circles.

A **polygon** is a closed figure whose sides are all line segments. Some examples of a polygon include an equilateral triangle, a square, and a pentagon.

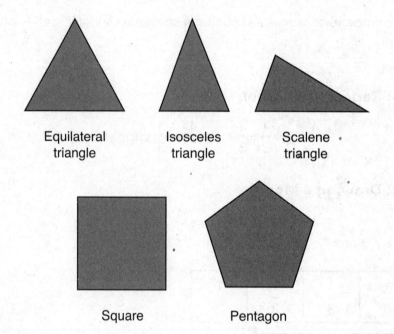

Equilateral triangle   Isosceles triangle   Scalene triangle

Square   Pentagon

A **triangle** is a polygon with three sides.

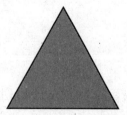

A **quadrilateral** is a polygon with four sides. Some examples of a quadrilateral include a trapezoid, a parallelogram, a rhombus, a rectangle, and a square.

A **circle** is not a polygon because it is a closed curve with all of its points in one plane and the same distance from a fixed point, which is referred to as the center.

Parallel sides are always the same distance apart like they are in the illustrations below.

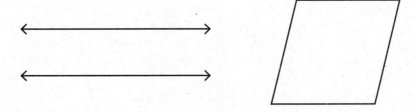

Perpendicular sides are formed when one line segment of a figure meets another line segment and forms a right angle (90°), as illustrated below.

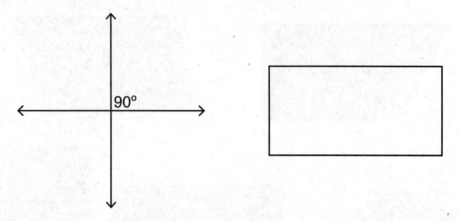

There are three types of **angle measures**: an **acute angle**, an **obtuse angle**, and a **right angle** as shown below.

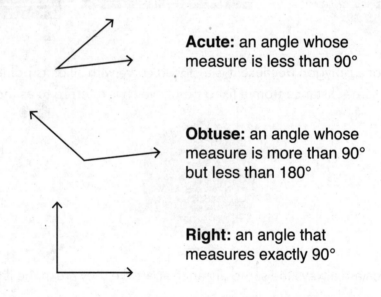

Acute: an angle whose measure is less than 90°

Obtuse: an angle whose measure is more than 90° but less than 180°

Right: an angle that measures exactly 90°

A **line of symmetry** is a line that divides a figure into figures that are mirror images of each other, as illustrated below.

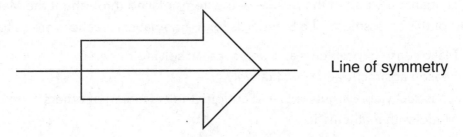

Line of symmetry

Common Core Domains and Mathematical Practices

The Math section of the Smarter Balanced Grade 4 assessment covers fewer topics in greater depth by focusing on the critical areas that were just reviewed. The test will require you to:

- use math concepts to solve problems;
- solve problems using your knowledge of concepts and problem-solving strategies;
- explain, justify, illustrate, and defend your reasoning about your solution to a problem; and
- use math models to symbolize a situation and recognize information/data from a real-life problem to solve it.

For the purposes of this book, we have made sure that all of the Common Core State Standards (CCSS) Domains are equally represented in the practice questions on our Math practice test. Those domains are:

- OA—Operations and Algebraic Thinking
- NBT—Number and Operations in Base Ten
- NF—Number and Operations—Fractions
- MD—Measurement and Data
- G—Geometry

See Appendix A at the back of this book for the full list of the Grade 4 Common Core State Standards.

The Common Core State Standards also require that full attention is given to the Standards for Mathematical Practices (SMP) within instruction and assessments. These standards are part of the design of the items placed throughout the Math portions of this assessment. The Standards for Mathematical Practices are as follows:

1. Make sense of problems and persevere in solving them.
2. Reason abstractly and quantitatively.
3. Construct viable arguments and critique the reasoning of others.
4. Model with mathematics.
5. Use appropriate tools strategically.
6. Attend to precision.
7. Look for and make use of structure.
8. Look for and express regularity in repeated reasoning.

See Appendix B at the back of this book for the full list of the Standards of Mathematical Practice.

Preparing for the Computer-Adaptive Test

CHAPTER 9

Overview

This chapter will provide you with an overview of the Math Computer-Adaptive Test (CAT) as well as show you strategies for answering CAT questions through guided practice.

The **Computer-Adaptive Test** is taken online and customizes a set of test questions just for you! Therefore, it is a more accurate measure of what you can do. There will be questions in a variety of formats that will be adapted, or adjusted, for you based on your answers to previous questions. If you answer a question correctly, then the next question will adjust to be harder than the previous question. On the other hand, if you answer a question incorrectly, then the next question will be adjusted to be easier than the previous question. The question formats for the CAT may require multiple-choice answers, constructed-response tasks (which are short, written answers), or technology-enhanced responses (which require you to select answers by clicking and highlighting a specific section or dragging and dropping the correct answer to a certain spot). All answers on the CAT are scored by a machine.

Math claims are summative statements about what you are predicted to show on the assessment. Table 9-1 outlines the Smarter Balanced Mathematical Claims.

Now, let's review some actual examples of Smarter Balanced questions that you might encounter on the Math CAT portion of the test. As you'll see, each example includes the claim, domain, student text, and evaluation rubrics, where applicable.

Table 9-1. Smarter Balanced Mathematical Claims

Claim #1—Concepts & Procedures
"Students can explain and apply mathematical concepts and interpret and carry out mathematical procedures with precision and fluency."
Claim #2—Problem Solving
"Students can solve a range of complex well-posed problems in pure and applied mathematics, making productive use of knowledge and problem solving strategies."
Claim #3—Communicating Reasoning
"Students can clearly and precisely construct viable arguments to support their own reasoning and to critique the reasoning of others."
Claim #4—Modeling and Data Analysis
"Students can analyze complex, real-world scenarios and construct and use mathematical models to interpret and solve problems."

Table courtesy of *www.smarterbalanced.org*

Example 1

Claim 1: Concepts and Procedures

Domain: NBT

This set of place-value blocks represents a number. The value of this number can be represented in many different ways.

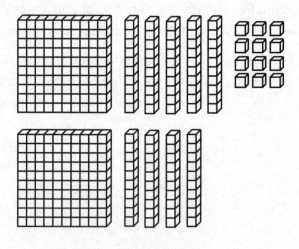

Key

⬚ = 1

For numbers 1a–1d, choose Yes or No to show whether the value is equivalent to the number represented by the place-value blocks.

1a.   200 + 90 + 12   O Yes   O No

1b.   Three hundred two   O Yes   O No

1c.   1 hundred + 20 tens + 2 ones   O Yes   O No

1d.   300 + 12   O Yes   O No

Scoring Rubric:

Responses to item will receive 0–2 points, based on the following:

2 points: YYYN—The student thoroughly understands place value in multi-digit whole numbers.

1 point: YYNN, YNYN, NYYN—The student partially understands place value in multi-digit whole numbers. The student does not fully understand that in multi-digit whole numbers values can be represented in word form, standard form, and expanded form, as well as in many other ways.

0 points: YYYY, YNNN, YNYY, YYNY, YNNY, NNNN, NYYY, NNYY, NNNY, NYNN, NNYN, NYNY—The student has little or inconsistent understanding of place value in multi-digit whole numbers. The student only answered one part correctly. **OR** The student thought the answer to 1d (which serves to confirm no understanding) was "Yes."

Example 2

Claim 2: Problem Solving

Domain: NF

A zookeeper made this line plot to show the ages of all the baboons at a zoo.

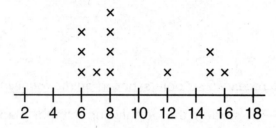

Baboon Ages (in years)

Part A

What fraction of the baboons at this zoo are eight years old?

$$\frac{\boxed{}}{\boxed{}}$$

Part B

What fraction of the baboons at this zoo are **<u>not</u>** 8 years old?

$$\frac{\boxed{}}{\boxed{}}$$

Sample Top-Score Response:

Each part of this task is scored separately and earns 1 point for a correct response.

Part A

$\frac{4}{12}$ or $\frac{1}{3}$

Part B

$\frac{8}{12}$ or $\frac{2}{3}$

SIDE NOTE FOR PROBLEM SOLVING

When you are trying to solve a problem, try these **S.T.A.R.** steps so that you can be a **STAR** problem solver!

1. **Stop**, read (and read again), and *understand* the problem. Ask yourself, "What do I know? What do I need to find out?"

2. **Think** about the *plan*, strategy, and tools you will use to solve the problem. Some strategies are:
   - Choose the operations needed.
   - Act it out.
   - Draw a picture, diagram, table, graph, or model.
   - Look for patterns.
   - Estimate.
   - Work backwards.

3. **Act.** Follow your plan and *solve the problem*. Make sure that you can explain how you solved the problem.

4. **Review** your answer. *Check*—did you answer the question? Can you explain why your answer is correct?

Example 3

Claim 3: Communicating Reasoning

Domain: OA

Peter made the statement shown below.

> "The number 32 is a multiple of 8. That means all of the factors of 8 are also factors of 32."

Is Peter's statement correct? In the space below, use numbers and words to explain why or why not?

Sample Top-Score Response:

Peter's statement is correct. The factors of 8 are 1, 2, 4, and 8. The factors of 32 are 1, 2, 4, 8, 16, and 32.

Scoring Rubric:

Responses to this item will receive 0−2 points, based on the following:

2 points: The student has a thorough understanding of the relationship between factors and multiples of numbers. The student correctly answers both parts and provides an explanation of reasoning that is thorough and correct for each part.

1 point: The student has a partial understanding of the relationship between factors and multiples of numbers. The student indicates that Peter's statement is correct, but provides an explanation of reasoning that is incomplete or contains a flaw.

0 points: The student has no understanding of the relationship between factors and multiples of numbers. The student does not complete any part correctly. Identifying Peter's statement as correct is not sufficient, by itself, to earn any credit.

Claim 4: Model and Data Analysis is tested on the Performance Task of the Grade 4 assessment, and the Performance Task example in Chapter 10 will focus on this claim.

You can also prepare for the CAT by working through the guided practice questions that follow in the next section of this chapter and by taking the Math practice test in Chapter 11. Also, reread the "How Can You Prepare" section in Chapter 2 to review a list of online resources that contain extra practice materials.

Guided Practice

The following five guided practice questions each represent an example of one of the five Common Core State Standards Domains for Grade 4. Remember, those domains are:

- OA—Operations and Algebraic Thinking
- NBT—Number and Operations in Base Ten
- NF—Number and Operations—Fractions
- MD—Measurement and Data
- G—Geometry

Practice Question 1

The following table shows the number of books in a school library for certain genres.

Genre	Number of Books
Science Fiction	493
Mystery	272
Adventure	511
Non-Fiction	626
Fantasy	350

Estimate the total number of books in all four genres. Enter your answer in the box below.

[   ] books

Answer: About 2,300 books

Explanation: Estimate each genre's number of books by rounding the number to the nearest hundred.

Genre	Number of Books	Number of Books Rounded to the Nearest Hundred
Science Fiction	493	500
Mystery	272	300
Adventure	511	500
Non-Fiction	626	600
Fantasy	350	400

Now, add up all of the rounded numbers to estimate the total number of books for all five genres.

$$500 + 300 + 500 + 600 + 400 = 2,300$$

Domain: OA—Operations and Algebraic Thinking

Practice Question 2

In the number 40,326, what does the 4 stand for? Choose **all** that apply.

- ☐ A. 4,000
- ☐ B. 4 [10,000s]
- ☐ C. 400,000
- ☐ D. 40,000

Answers: (B) and **(D)**

Explanation: The 4 in 40,326 is worth 40,000. Choice A is incorrect because the 4 is worth 4,000, which is 10 times less than 40,000. Choice B is correct because 4 [10,000] is equal to 40,000. Choice C is incorrect because the 4 is worth 400,000, which is ten times more than 40,000. Choice D is correct because the 4 is worth 40,000.

Domain: NBT—Number and Operations in Base Ten

Practice Question 3

Figure A below has $\frac{3}{12}$ of its whole shaded.

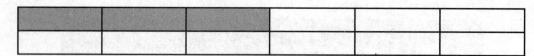

Figure A

In the box below, enter another fraction that is equivalent to $\frac{3}{12}$.

Answer: Answers will vary. Possible answers include $\frac{1}{4}$, $\frac{6}{24}$, $\frac{9}{36}$, or any other fraction that is equivalent to $\frac{3}{12}$.

Explanation: To find an equivalent of a fraction, the numerator and denominator of the original fraction must be multiplied or divided by the same number. In this example, $3 \div 3 = 1$ and $12 \div 3 = 4$, so $\dfrac{3}{12} = \dfrac{1}{4}$. Also, since $3 \times 2 = 6$ and $12 \times 2 = 24$, $\dfrac{3}{12} = \dfrac{6}{24}$.

Domain: NF—Number and Operations—Fractions

Practice Question 4

Wesley is putting in a vegetable garden and wants to put a fence around it. The area of the garden, in yards, is shown below.

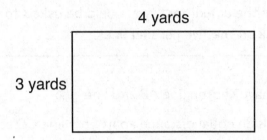

4 yards

3 yards

How many feet of fence should Wesley purchase? Enter your answer, in **feet**, in the box below.

feet

Answer: 42 feet

Explanation: The garden in this question is measured in yards, but these measurements need to be converted to feet in order to answer the question. The perimeter of the garden is 14 yards (4 yards + 4 yards + 3 yards + 3 yards). Since there are 3 feet in 1 yard, multiply 14 × 3 to find the answer of 42 feet.

Domain: MD—Measurement and Data

Practice Question 5

In the figure below, choose which two lines are parallel.

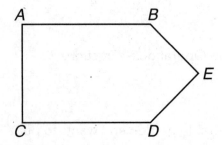

Note that, on the actual test, you would be asked to use your mouse to click on the two parallel lines.

Answer: You should have chosen line *AB* and line *CD*.

Explanation: Line *AB* is an equal distance apart from line *CD* at all points.

Domain: G—Geometry

Preparing for the Performance Task

CHAPTER 10

Overview

This chapter will provide you with an overview of the Math Performance Task (PT) as well as show you strategies for answering Performance Task questions through guided practice.

For the Math **Performance Task**, you will be asked to apply your math knowledge and skills by responding to a real-world situation. The task will be connected to a theme or scenario that your teacher will introduce to you in the Classroom Activity. Then, you will answer multi-step questions and perform activities with many parts that deal with that theme or scenario.

The role of the PT is to provide you with the opportunity to apply your learning in context. The PT also serves as evidence of your learning. Basically, it gives you a chance to show what you know! Your performance on this task will measure your achievement and academic growth, while allowing for multiple approaches. That is because some items may require hand-scoring with the use of rubrics that are based on specific criteria.

There are three important steps involved in the Performance Task. First, you will work on the **Classroom Activity**. This activity takes about 25−30 minutes and is NOT scored. The goal is to ensure that all students have a common understanding of the theme or scenario that is being discussed. During this activity, your teacher will introduce you to the topic, any unfamiliar concepts that are associated with the topic, and important terms you might need to know in order to complete the task. This activity is meant to be engaging and motivating while also introducing new vocabulary, building background knowledge of the theme or scenario, and creating context for the task at hand. Next is the **Stimulus**, which is the scenario or situation that will be read by you. The stimulus contains data that you will need to complete the task. Finally, you will work on the **Performance Task** itself, which consists of a few questions based on the information learned in the previous steps. There will likely be several variations of the same task, so you and your classmates may not answer the exact same questions.

155

The **Equation Response Editorial Tool** is a tool that will be provided to help you enter answers that are numbers, expressions, or equations. This tool is NOT a calculator. You will need to perform your own calculations on scrap paper and then use the tool only to input your responses. An example of this tool is presented in Figure 10-1 below.

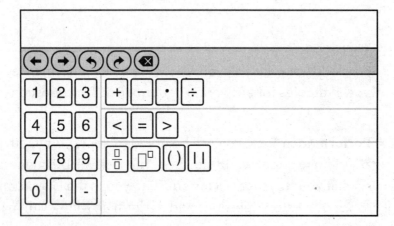

Figure 10-1. Equation Response Editorial Tool

To better familiarize yourself with the Equation Response Editorial Tool, visit the following website: *https://demo.tds.airast.org/eqtutorial/*

Guided Practice

The Performance Task portion of this assessment exemplifies the Smarter Balanced Mathematical Claim 4, which states that "students can analyze complex, real-world scenarios and can construct and use mathematical models to interpret and solve problems." The following practice Performance Task will illustrate this claim.

> ### NOTE
>
> This practice Performance Task does not contain a Classroom Activity. This Performance Task is just designed to provide you with practice answering the questions on the actual Performance Task. There will be a full Performance Task, complete with a Classroom Activity, on the Math practice test in Chapter 11.

Practice Performance Task

Budgeting Money

Christine works at a part-time job. She earns $9 for each hour that she works. She would like to budget her money so that she can purchase the following items with her earnings.

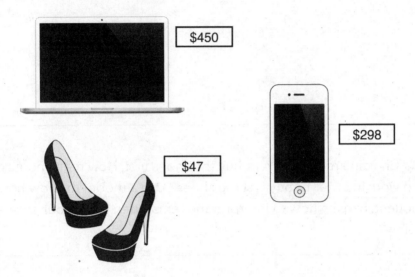

$450

$298

$47

1. Christine needs to know the amount of time that it will take her to earn enough money to buy the items above.

   Part A: How many hours does Christine need to work in order to earn enough money to buy the computer? Use place value and mental math to solve. Enter your answer in the box below.

Part B: How many hours does Christine need to work to buy the shoes and the phone? Explain how to interpret the remainder. Enter your answer in the box below.

Part C: Christine really wants to buy the shoes first. How many hours does she need to work in order to buy just the shoes? Use a model to show how to find the quotient. Explain how to interpret the remainder. Enter your answer in the box below.

Sample Responses

Part A

Answer: 50 hours

Explanation: The computer costs $450. Christine makes $9 for each hour that she works. Therefore, you will need to divide 450 by 9. There are two ways of thinking of this.

$$\$450 \div 9 = 50 \text{ hours}$$

or

$$45 \text{ tens} \div 9 \text{ tens} = 5 \text{ tens or } 50 \text{ hours}$$

Scoring Rubric: 2 points if both the answer and the strategy are correct. 1 point if only the answer, or only the strategy, is correct.

Part B

Answer: 39 hours

Explanation: The shoes cost $47, and the phone costs $298. Added together, the total cost for both the shoes and the phone is $345. Remember, Christine earns $9 for every hour that she works. Therefore, you need to divide 345 by 9.

$$345 \div 9 = 38R3$$

After 38 hours, Christine will only have made $342, which is not enough to buy both items. The remainder, 3, indicates that she needs to work one additional hour, which means that she needs to work 39 hours total to purchase both items.

Scoring Rubric: 2 points if both the answer and the explanation are correct. 1 point if only the answer, or only the explanation, is correct.

Part C

Answer: 6 hours

Explanation: The shoes cost $47. Christine earns $9 for each hour that she works. Divide 47 by 9 to find out how many hours she needs to work to buy just the shoes.

$$47 \div 9 = 5R2$$

A sample model would look like:

```
000000000
000000000
000000000
000000000
000000000
00
```

After 5 hours, Christine will only have made $45, which is not enough money to buy the shoes. The remainder, 2, tells you that Christine needs to work another hour. Therefore, Christine needs to work 6 hours total to earn enough money to buy just the shoes.

Scoring Rubric: 3 points if the answer, model, and explanation are all correct. 2 points if only 2 of the 3 items (the answer, the model, and the explanation) are correct. 1 point if only 1 of the 3 items (the answer, the model, and the explanation) is correct.

Math Practice Test

Computer-Adaptive Test

Directions: The following practice test is similar to the one given by the Smarter Balanced Assessment Consortium (SBAC). The actual CAT assessment will be given on a computer and is adaptive. This means that there will be a set of questions, in a variety of formats, that will be customized to you based on your answers to previous questions. For the purposes of this preparation guide, the questions on this test are representative of the kinds of technology-enhanced questions on the actual assessment. These test questions include a variety of difficulty levels ranging from easier to more difficult examples.

This test contains 45 questions. The number of questions on the actual test may vary. Be sure to read each question carefully and answer every part of each question as completely as possible.

1. Select the statement below that correctly explains how the values of the numbers 480 and 4,800 are different.

   O A. 4,800 is 1,000 times as large as 480.
   O B. 4,800 is 10 times as large as 480.
   O C. 4,800 is 100 times as large as 480.
   O D. 4,800 is 1 time as large as 480.

2. The cost of buying a concert ticket is 6 times the cost of purchasing a CD. It costs $18 to buy a CD. What is the cost, in dollars, of purchasing a concert ticket? Enter your answer in the box below.

   $ [   ]

3. Decide if each fraction is equal to $\frac{3}{4}$. In the table below, place an X in the YES column if the fraction is equal or place an X in the NO column if the fraction is not equal.

Fraction	YES	NO
$\frac{6}{8}$		
$\frac{1}{2}$		
$\frac{9}{12}$		

4. Place an X in the box that matches each figure with its description. Each figure can have more than one matched description.

	Has at Least One Right Angle	Has at Least One Pair of Perpendicular Sides	Has at Least One Pair of Parallel Sides
Rectangle			
Triangle			
Parallelogram			

5. Enter the length, in **millimeters**, of the following pencil in the box below.

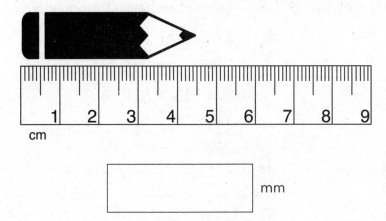

cm

| | mm

6. The town's baseball team has been keeping statistics on how many games they have won over the past 7 years. Use their bar chart below to answer Part A and Part B.

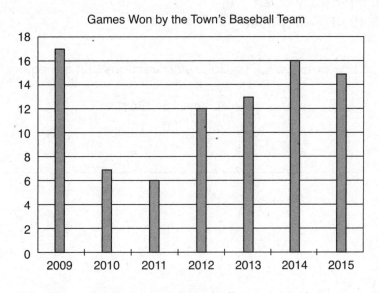

Part A: In what year did the town's baseball team win the most games? Enter your answer in the box below.

Part B: How many more games did the town's baseball team win in 2014 than they did in 2010? Enter your answer in the box below.

7. Which number, when filled into each of the empty boxes below, makes each equation true? Enter your answer in the box below the equations.

$$3 \times \square = 21$$
$$\square \times 3 = 21$$
$$21 \div \square = 3$$
$$21 \div 3 = \square$$

8. Place an X in the box of the number name for 673.

- ☐ Six hundred sixty-three
- ☐ Six hundred seven three
- ☐ Six hundred thirty-seven
- ☐ Six hundred seventy-three

9. Write in the box below, all of the following fractions that are equivalent to $\frac{3}{4}$.

$$\frac{9}{12}, \frac{1}{4}, \frac{6}{8}, \frac{15}{20}, \frac{34}{14}$$

10. A garden hose is 12 yards long. What is its length in **inches**? Enter your answer in the box below.

inches

11. From the following list of equations, choose **all** of the equations that will have an even product.

   ☐ A. $32 \times 2 =$
   ☐ B. $91 \times 3 =$
   ☐ C. $67 \times 4 =$
   ☐ D. $84 \times 5 =$
   ☐ E. $43 \times 6 =$

12. Which of the following numbers round to 300,000 when rounded to the nearest hundred thousand? Choose **all** that apply.

   ☐ A. 1,996,324
   ☐ B. 280,093
   ☐ C. 226,000
   ☐ D. 259,960
   ☐ E. 312,001

13. Last week, Christine ran $2\frac{1}{8}$ miles on Monday and $4\frac{5}{8}$ miles on Wednesday.

   Part A: How many miles did Christine run in total last week? Enter your answer in the box below.

   | | miles |

   Part B: How many more miles did she run on Wednesday than she ran on Monday? Enter your answer in the box below.

   | | miles |

14. Jamal's swim practice started at 3:45 P.M. and ended at 5:15 P.M. How long did his swim practice last? Write the correct answer into the answer box.

   1 hour, 30 minutes   1 hour, 15 minutes   1 hour, 45 minutes

15. What is the perimeter (*P*) and area (*A*) of the following figure?

12 inches

10 inches

P = [   ] inches

A = [   ] inches squared

16. Use any strategy to find the quotient of the problem below.

$9,729 \div 9 =$ ----------------

17. Write the numbers below into their correct classification.

| 11 | 8 | 3 | 21 | 48 | 17 | 81 |

Prime	Composite

18. Choose **all** of the comparisons below that are true.

- ☐ A. 203,672 > 201,999
- ☐ B. 990,000 < 999,000
- ☐ C. 578 > 4,326
- ☐ D. 831 + 6 > 837
- ☐ E. 126,734 < 127,634

19. Mrs. Clarke's guided reading group was reading a novel. After the first week, she checked with her students to see how much of the book they had each read. Mrs. Clarke recorded the fraction of the book that four of her students had read. Her results are in the table below.

Student	Fraction of the Book Read
Isabella	$\frac{1}{3}$
Maya	$\frac{3}{4}$
Juan	$\frac{2}{6}$
Chris	$\frac{2}{3}$

Part A: Who read the greatest fraction of the book after the first week? Enter your answer in the box below.

Part B: Which two students read the same amount of the book in the first week? Enter your answer in the box below.

20. Eileen has a piggy bank full of quarters, dimes, nickels, and pennies. Choose **all** of the combinations that she could use to make $1.08.

☐ A. 4 quarters, 1 nickel, 3 pennies
☐ B. 10 dimes, 2 nickels, 3 pennies
☐ C. 3 quarters, 3 dimes, 3 pennies
☐ D. 2 quarters, 5 dimes, 1 nickel, 3 pennies

21. Choose YES or NO to say if each sentence is true.

A. $1,865 \times 4 = 7,560$ O Yes   O No
B. $9,378 - 2,536 = 6,842$ O Yes   O No
C. $2,826 \div 3 = 942$ O Yes   O No
D. $24,508 = 12,211 + 11,298$ O Yes   O No

22. Michelle is making 18 gift bags for her friends who will attend her birthday party. She places 24 items in each bag. How many items will Michelle use in all to make her gift bags? Enter your answer in the box below.

	items

23. Write the fractions at their correct place on the number line below.

$$\frac{5}{6} \qquad \frac{2}{6} \qquad \frac{1}{2} \qquad \frac{6}{6}$$

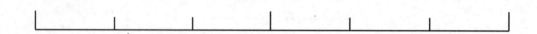

24. Choose YES or NO to say if the fraction is greater than $\frac{3}{5}$.

A. $\frac{3}{3}$ O Yes   O No

B. $\frac{2}{5}$ O Yes   O No

C. $\frac{3}{8}$ O Yes   O No

D. $\frac{3}{4}$ O Yes   O No

25. A pizza was cut into equal parts. Fifteen pieces of the pie were eaten. The three remaining pieces equaled an angle of 60°. What was the angle of one piece of pizza? Enter your answer in the box below.

$$\boxed{} \ °$$

26. Mia's car is 4 meters long. How many **centimeters** long is Mia's car? Enter your answer in the box below.

$$\boxed{} \ \text{centimeters}$$

27. Which of the following sets contains all of the factors of 72?

○ A. 1, 2, 4, 8, 9, 18, 36, 72
○ B. 1, 3, 4, 6, 8, 9, 12, 18, 24, 72
○ C. 1, 2, 3, 4, 6, 8, 9, 12, 18, 24, 36, 72
○ D. 1, 2, 8, 9, 36, 72

28. For the town yard sale, there were 2,316 board games, 593 items of clothing, and 1,890 video games donated. How many games were donated to the yard sale? Enter your answer in the box below.

$$\boxed{} \ \text{games}$$

29. Choose **all** of the expressions that have an estimated quotient of 700 when the dividend is rounded to the hundreds place.

   O A. 2,792 ÷ 4
   O B. 5,366 ÷ 9
   O C. 5,619 ÷ 8
   O D. 2,052 ÷ 3

30. Which addition sentence does the following model show?

  +

_____ + _____ = _____

31. Choose the BEST estimate for 248 ÷ 3.

   O A.   250 ÷ 5 = 50
   O B.   240 ÷ 3 = 80
   O C.   300 ÷ 3 = 100
   O D.   200 ÷ 5 = 40

32. Find the missing numbers in this multiplication problem. Enter the missing numbers in the empty boxes.

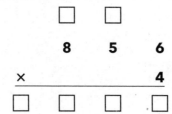

33. Juanita measured the growth of her plant. Her results are recorded below.

- In week one, it grew $1\frac{1}{2}$ inches.

- In week two, it grew $3\frac{3}{4}$ inches.

- In week three, it grew $2\frac{1}{4}$ inches.

How many inches did her plant grow during these three weeks?

- O A. $6\frac{3}{4}$ inches

- O B. $7\frac{1}{2}$ inches

- O C. $8\frac{1}{4}$ inches

- O D. $7\frac{3}{4}$ inches

34. A movie lasted $3\frac{1}{2}$ hours. How many minutes did the movie last?

- O A. 180 minutes
- O B. 60 minutes
- O C. 210 minutes
- O D. 330 minutes

35. Manny wants to paint his bedroom. His dad tells him that he will need $\frac{3}{5}$ gallon of paint for each of the 4 walls. How much paint will Manny need in total? Choose two of the amounts below that are equivalent to what amount of paint Manny will need.

- ☐ A. $\frac{12}{5}$

- ☐ B. $\frac{12}{20}$

- ☐ C. $2\frac{2}{5}$

36. Write the following fractions into the correct space.

$$\frac{5}{8} \qquad \frac{3}{8} \qquad \frac{4}{12} \qquad \frac{8}{16} \qquad \frac{2}{3} \qquad \frac{5}{10}$$

Less than $\frac{1}{2}$	Equal to $\frac{1}{2}$	Greater than $\frac{1}{2}$

37. Choose all of the rectangles below that have an area of 24. Circle your answers.

38. Write each measure below to match the given measure in the table.

7 yd   10,000 lb   32 fl oz   6 ft

4 c	
	5 T
72 in	
	21 ft

39. Choose YES or NO to say if the equation is correct.

A. 2 l = 200 ml   O Yes   O No

B. 3 yd = 12 ft   O Yes   O No

C. 4 kg = 4,000 g   O Yes   O No

D. 7 cm = 70 mm   O Yes   O No

40. Trevor wrote the following equation to find an angle measure of a circle.

$$360° \div a = b$$

What do the variables, *a* and *b*, represent in Trevor's equation? Write *a* or *b* in the boxes below next to what each variable represents.

☐ The number of degrees in each part by which the circle is divided

☐ The number of equal parts into which the circle is divided

41. Which of the following geometric terms describes angle *MAG* below?

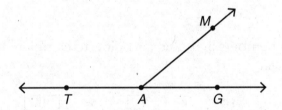

O A. Obtuse

O B. Acute

O C. Straight

O D. Right

42. Hans created the following multiplication table.

×	6	7	8	9
9	54	63	72	81
10	60	70	80	90
11	66	77	88	99
12	73	84	96	108

After creating the table, he realized that he made one mistake. Which fact did Hans get wrong? Enter your answer in the box below.

43. Write the correct numbers in the boxes below to complete the area model and the equation shown.

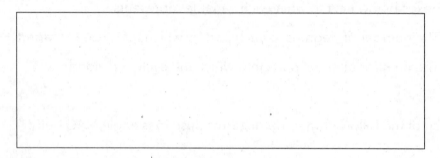

44. Write the correct numbers in the boxes below to complete the area model and the equation shown.

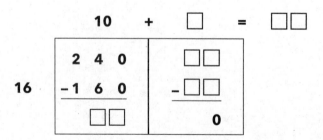

45. Mr. Santiago wants to buy 270 hot dog rolls and 350 hamburger rolls for the end-of-the-year company barbeque. Both types of rolls are sold in packages of 8.

Part A: How many packages of hot dog rolls must Mr. Santiago buy? Write an equation using the letter *h* for the unknown amount. Then, solve the equation. If there is a remainder, put it in fraction form. Enter your answer in the box below.

Part B: How many packages of hamburger rolls must Mr. Santiago buy? Write an equation using the letter *b* for the unknown amount. Then, solve the equation. If there is a remainder, put it in fraction form. Enter your answer in the box below.

Part C: One package of either type of roll each costs $4.00. Based on your answers to Parts A and B, how much will Mr. Santiago spend on rolls for the barbeque? Enter your answer in the box below.

Performance Task

Classroom Activity

Note that when completing this classroom activity, you should ask your parent or teacher to serve as the "facilitator" and read those parts aloud to you.

Resources Needed

- Whiteboard, notebook, paper, or some other similar material for recording your responses
- Projector, computer monitor, or some other similar device for viewing photographs
- A computer with Wi-Fi that can be used for searching images

Learning Goals

- To understand what a pastry chef is
- To become familiar with the products that are mentioned in this task (i.e., cookies, cupcakes, eclairs, tarts, Danish pastries)
- To understand how these pastry products might be displayed in a pastry shop or packaged in different size boxes

Setting the Context

Facilitator: "Do you know what a pastry chef is?"

(The facilitator waits for a response. The student should say whether or not he or she has ever heard of this term before.)

Facilitator: "A pastry chef or *patissier* is a master baker and dessert artist. He or she makes fancy cakes, breads, and other treats. Have you ever been to a pastry shop before? If so, when and where?"

(The facilitator waits for a response. The student should answer whether he or she has ever been to a pastry shop before. If the answer is yes, the student should state when he or she visited the pastry shop and where it was located.)

Facilitator: "What pastry items do you know of?"

(The facilitator waits for a response. Together, the facilitator and the student should make a list, and, if necessary, the facilitator should introduce any examples that the student does not know. Examples of pastry items include: cupcakes, eclairs, tarts, cookies, Danish pastries, pies, soufflés, truffles, croissants, etc. The facilitator should then show the student the following five pictures of pastry examples.)

Facilitator: "Do you know how pastry shops might package their treats when they sell them to their customers?"

(The facilitator waits for a response. Together, the facilitator and the student should make a list of the different ways that a pastry shop might package these products. If necessary, the facilitator should introduce examples of different ways. Some examples include: boxes of different sizes depending on the items sold, bags of different sizes, etc. The facilitator should then show the student the following picture of different size pastry boxes.]

(The facilitator could then complete any of the following four actions to help students understand this task better:

- Visit a pastry shop.
- Conduct an online search of examples of pastry shops.
- Conduct an online search of examples of pastries.
- Conduct an online search of examples of pastry boxes.)

Facilitator: "Now that you are familiar with a pastry shop, you are going to apply this knowledge to a task on your own. You are now ready to begin a Performance Task where you will first help a pastry shop decide how many boxes it will need for its treats, then create a plan for a cupcake display, and finally determine how much the customers will get charged for certain orders."

Performance Task

The Pastry Chef

Stephanie's family owns a pastry shop in town. It specializes in making cookies, cupcakes, eclairs, tarts, and Danish pastries. You will first help her decide how many boxes she will need for her treats. Then, you will create a plan for a cupcake display. Finally, you will determine how much the customers will get charged for certain orders. Record your answers for each part in the space provided. The following table shows each item, the amount of that item that fits in one box, and the price per item. Use the information in the table to help answer the questions.

Item	Amount That Fits in One Box	Price Per Item (tax included)
Cookies	24	$0.75
Cupcakes	12	$2.50
Eclairs	6	$3.00
Tarts	2	$3.25
Danish pastries	4	$1.50

1. Decide how many boxes she needs for her treats.

As the pastry chef, Stephanie makes 48 of each of these items every weekday.

Part A: How many boxes does Stephanie need for each item each weekday? Fill in the chart below to show your responses.

Item	Number of Boxes Needed
Cookies	
Cupcakes	
Eclairs	
Tarts	
Danish pastries	

Part B: Justify your answers to Part A by writing two equations that you could use to determine how many boxes are needed for each item every weekday.

Item	Equations Used
Cookies	
Cupcakes	
Eclairs	
Tarts	
Danish pastries	

Part C: How many total boxes does Stephanie need each weekday? Solve and explain your answer in the box below.

Part D: Choose whether each statement below is true or false.

The amount of eclairs made per day and the amount of tarts made per day are both multiples of 8.   ○ True   ○ False

Danish pastries fill the most boxes.   ○ True   ○ False

The number of boxes needed for each item is always an even number.   ○ True   ○ False

2. Create a plan for a cupcake display.

On Saturday, the pastry shop will cater a birthday party with a cupcake display.

Part A: Help Stephanie determine the number of trays that she will need to display the cupcakes for the party. Each tray can hold 10 cupcakes. $\frac{8}{10}$ of a tray will be vanilla cupcakes. $\frac{9}{10}$ of a tray will be chocolate cupcakes. $\frac{6}{10}$ of a tray will be red velvet cupcakes. $\frac{5}{10}$ of a tray will be peanut butter cupcakes. $\frac{9}{5}$ of a tray will be rainbow sprinkle cupcakes. How many trays will be needed in total?

Illustrate your display by writing each tray into the workspace below. Then write the initials of each cupcake (V = vanilla, C = chocolate, RV = red velvet, PB = peanut butter, RS = rainbow sprinkles) onto the trays to reflect the information above. Be sure to fill each tray completely before beginning another. Note that some trays and initials may not be used.

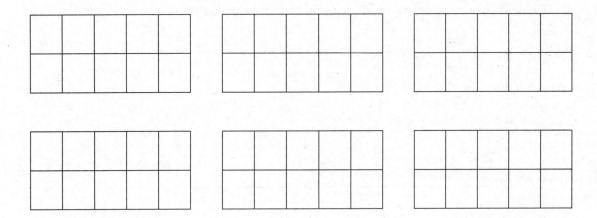

V V V V V V V V V V V

C C C C C C C C C C C C

RV RV RV RV RV RV RV RV RV RV RV RV

PB PB PB PB PB PB PB PB PB PB PB PB

RS RS RS RS RS RS RS RS RS RS RS RS RS RS
RS RS RS RS RS RS RS RS RS RS

---------------- trays are needed.

Part B: What fractional part of the last tray can still be filled with cupcakes? Explain your answer, using an equation, in the box below.

Part C: Are there more chocolate or rainbow sprinkle cupcakes in the display? Complete the response below.

There are more _____ cupcakes because _____

_____

_____

3. Determine how much the customers will get charged for certain orders.

Part A: Refer back to the information about the cost of cupcakes at the start of the Performance Task as well as the information about cupcake display in Question 2. If the display was billed out per cupcake, how much did the cupcake display cost for the birthday party? Explain your answer in the box below.

Part B: Every Wednesday, the local garden club orders 2 dozen cookies, 12 eclairs, and 10 tarts for its weekly meeting. How much does the club get charged each week? If the garden club always pays with a $100 bill, how much change do they receive? Explain both of your answers in the boxes below.

Total for the weekly order = $ --------------------------

Change received = $ --------------------------

Computer-Adaptive Test, page 161

1. **(B)** $480 \times 10 = 4{,}800$. Choices A, C, and D do not correctly explain how the values of the numbers 480 and 4,800 are different.

   Domain: NBT—Number and Operations in Base Ten

2. **$108** The question tells you that it costs $18 to buy a CD, and it is 6 times as much to purchase a concert ticket. Therefore, multiply $18 times 6 to find the cost of a concert ticket.

$$\$18 \times 6 = \$108$$

   Domain: OA—Operations and Algebraic Thinking

3. Your table should read as follows:

Fraction	YES	NO
$\frac{6}{8}$	X	
$\frac{1}{2}$		X
$\frac{9}{12}$	X	

To find an equivalent of a fraction, the numerator and the denominator of the original fraction must be multiplied or divided by the same number.

$\frac{3}{4} = \frac{6}{8}$. If you multiply the original numerator, 3, by 2, you get the new numerator, 6. If you multiply the original denominator, 4, by 2, you get the new denominator, 8.

$\frac{3}{4} \neq \frac{1}{2}$. There is no possible number to multiply or divide the original numerator and denominator by to get that combination. Also, the original numerator, 3, is not half of the original denominator, 4.

$\frac{3}{4} = \frac{9}{12}$. If you multiply the original numerator, 3, by 3, you get the new numerator, 9. If you multiply the original denominator, 4, by 3, you get the new denominator, 12.

Domain: NF—Number and Operations—Fractions

4. Your table should read as follows:

	Has at Least One Right Angle	Has at Least One Pair of Perpendicular Sides	Has at Least One Pair of Parallel Sides
Rectangle	X	X	X
Triangle	X	X	
Parallelogram			X

A rectangle contains four right angles (90° angles), has more than one pair of perpendicular sides, and has two pairs of parallel sides, meaning that all three descriptions in the table are reflective of a rectangle. The triangle shown contains one right angle and has one pair of perpendicular sides. It does not contain at least one pair of parallel sides. Therefore, only the first two descriptions in the table are reflective of this triangle. A parallelogram does not contain any right angles nor does it contain any perpendicular sides. It does, however, contain two pairs of parallel sides. Therefore, only the third description in the table is reflective of the parallelogram.

Domain: G—Geometry

5. **45 mm** The pencil in this question measures 4.5 centimeters. There are 10 millimeters in 1 centimeter. Therefore, multiply 4.5 by 10 to find out the length of the pencil in millimeters.

$$4.5 \times 10 = 45$$

Domain: MD—Measurement and Data

6. **Part A: 2009** Looking at the bar graph, you can see that the bar for the year 2009 is longest. It ends half way between 16 and 18, which means that, in 2009, the town's baseball team won 17 games. This is more than any of the other years represented.

Part B: 9 The bar graph shows that the team won 16 games in 2014. It also shows that the team won 7 games in 2010. The difference between 16 and 7 $(16 - 7)$ is 9.

Domain: MD—Measurement and Data

7. **7** See the completed equations below.

$$3 \times 7 = 21$$
$$7 \times 3 = 21$$
$$21 \div 7 = 3$$
$$21 \div 3 = 7$$

Domain: OA—Operations and Algebraic Thinking

8. You should have placed an **X** in the box next to **Six hundred seventy-three**.

Domain: NBT—Number and Operations in Base Ten

9. The fractions that are equivalent to $\frac{3}{4}$ are $\frac{9}{12}$, $\frac{6}{8}$, and $\frac{15}{20}$. This is because:

$$\frac{9}{12} \div \frac{3}{3} = \frac{3}{4}$$

$$\frac{6}{8} \div \frac{2}{2} = \frac{3}{4}$$

$$\frac{15}{20} \div \frac{5}{5} = \frac{3}{4}$$

Domain: NF—Number and Operations—Fractions

10. **432 inches** The garden hose is 12 yards long. There are 36 inches in 1 yard. Therefore, $36 \times 12 = 432$ inches.

You could also solve this problem using partial products as shown below:

$$
\begin{array}{r}
36 \\
\times\ 12 \\
\hline
12 \\
60 \\
60 \\
+300 \\
\hline
432
\end{array}
\qquad
\begin{array}{l}
2 \times 6 = 12 \\
2 \times 30 = 60 \\
10 \times 6 = 60 \\
10 \times 30 = 300
\end{array}
$$

Domain: MD—Measurement and Data

11. **(A)**, **(C)**, **(D)**, and **(E)** Below are the products for each answer choice.

    A. $32 \times 2 = 64$ (EVEN)

    B. $91 \times 3 = 273$ (ODD)

    C. $67 \times 4 = 268$ (EVEN)

    D. $84 \times 5 = 420$ (EVEN)

    E. $43 \times 6 = 258$ (EVEN)

Domain: OA—Operations and Algebraic Thinking

12. **(B)**, **(D)**, and **(E)** Below are each of the choices rounded to the nearest hundred thousand.

    A. $1{,}996{,}324 \rightarrow 2{,}000{,}000$ (NO)

    B. $280{,}093 \rightarrow 300{,}000$ (YES)

    C. $226{,}000 \rightarrow 200{,}000$ (NO)

    D. $259{,}960 \rightarrow 300{,}000$ (YES)

    E. $312{,}001 \rightarrow 300{,}000$ (YES)

Domain: NBT—Number and Operations in Base Ten

13. **Part A:** $6\dfrac{6}{8}$ or $6\dfrac{3}{4}$ Add the two amounts of miles that Christine ran on

    Monday and Wednesday to find the total number of miles.

    $$2\dfrac{1}{8} + 4\dfrac{5}{8} = 6 + \dfrac{6}{8} = 6\dfrac{6}{8} \text{ or } 6\dfrac{3}{4} \text{ in simplest form}$$

    Part B: $2\dfrac{4}{8}$ or $2\dfrac{1}{2}$ Subtract the number of miles Christine ran on Monday from

    the number of miles that she ran on Wednesday.

    $$4\dfrac{5}{8} - 2\dfrac{1}{8} = 2 + \dfrac{4}{8} = 2\dfrac{4}{8} \text{ or } 2\dfrac{1}{2} \text{ in simplest form}$$

    Domain: NF—Number and Operations—Fractions

14. **1 hour, 30 minutes** Jamal's practice started at 3:45. One hour then passed, making it 4:45. Then, another 30 minutes passed until the end at 5:15.

    Domain: MD—Measurement and Data

15. *P* **= 44 inches** and *A* **= 120 inches squared**

    To find the perimeter, add up all the sides: $P = 12 + 12 + 10 + 10 = 44$ inches

    To find the area, multiply the length times the height: $A = 12 \times 10 = 120$ inches squared

    Domain: MD—Measurement and Data

16. **1,081**

    $$9,729 \div 9 = 1,081$$

    Domain: NBT—Number and Operations in Base Ten

17. Your tables should read as follows:

Prime	Composite
3	8
11	21
17	48
	81

A prime number is a number that only has 1 and itself as factors. For example:

$$1 \times 3 = 3$$

$$1 \times 11 = 11$$

$$1 \times 17 = 17$$

A composite number is a number that has more than two factors. For example:

The factors of 8 are: 1, 2, 4, and 8

The factors of 21 are: 1, 3, 7, and 21

The factors of 48 are: 1, 2, 3, 4, 6, 8, 12, 16, 24, and 48

The factors of 81 are: 1, 3, 9, 27, and 81

Domain: OA—Operations and Algebraic Thinking

18. **(A)**, **(B)**, and **(E)**

    A. 203,672 > 201,999 (YES)

    B. 990,000 < 999,000 (YES)

    C. 578 > 4,326 (NO—578 is less than 4,326)

    D. 831 + 6 > 837 (NO—831 + 6 is equal to 837)

    E. 126,734 < 127,634 (YES)

Domain: NBT—Number and Operations in Base Ten

19. **Part A: Maya** read the greatest fraction of the book after the first week.

$$\frac{1}{3} = 0.\overline{3}$$

$$\frac{3}{4} = 0.75$$

$$\frac{2}{6} = 0.\overline{3}$$

$$\frac{2}{3} = 0.\overline{6}$$

Part B: Isabella and **Juan** read the same amount of the book in the first week.

$$\frac{1 \times 2}{3 \times 2} = \frac{2}{6}$$

Domain: NF—Number and Operations—Fractions

20. **(A)**, **(C)**, and **(D)**

   A. 4 quarters, 1 nickel, 3 pennies = 1.00 + 0.05 + 0.03 = \$1.08

   B. 10 dimes, 2 nickels, 3 pennies = 1.00 + 0.10 + 0.03 = \$1.13

   C. 3 quarters, 3 dimes, 3 pennies = 0.75 + 0.30 + 0.03 = \$1.08

   D. 2 quarters, 5 dimes, 1 nickel, 3 pennies = 0.50 + 0.50 + 0.05 + 0.03 = \$1.08

   Domain: MD—Measurement and Data

21. **(A)** and **(D)** are both **NO**. **(B)** and **(C)** are both **YES**.

   A. $1{,}865 \times 4 \neq 7{,}560$ (No. $1{,}865 \times 4 = 7{,}460$.)

   B. $9{,}378 - 2{,}536 = 6{,}842$ (Yes, this is correct.)

   C. $2{,}826 \div 3 = 942$ (Yes, this is correct.)

   D. $24{,}508 = 12{,}211 + 11{,}298$ (No. $12{,}211 + 11{,}298 = 23{,}509$.)

   Domain: OA—Operations and Algebraic Thinking

22. **432 items** Michelle is making 18 gift bags. There are 24 items in each gift bag. Therefore, to find the total, multiply 18 by 24.

$$18 \times 24 = 432$$

Another way to solve this problem would be by using partial products as shown below.

Partial Products Example

$$
\begin{array}{r}
18 \\
\times\ 24 \\
\hline
32 \\
40 \\
160 \\
+200 \\
\hline
432
\end{array}
$$

   $4 \times 8 = 32$
   $4 \times 10 = 40$
   $20 \times 8 = 160$
   $20 \times 10 = 200$

   Domain: NBT—Number and Operations in Base Ten

23. Your number line should match the one below.

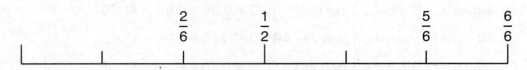

Domain: NF—Number and Operations—Fractions

24. **(A)** and **(D)** are both **YES**. **(B)** and **(C)** are both **NO**.

A. $\frac{3}{3} > \frac{3}{5}$ (Yes. $\frac{3}{3}$ is equal to 1 whole, so $\frac{3}{5}$ must be less than 1 whole.)

B. $\frac{2}{5} > \frac{3}{5}$ (No. 2 out of 5 is less than, not greater than, 3 out of 5.)

C. $\frac{3}{8} > \frac{3}{5}$ (No. Convert each fraction to an equivalent fraction so that both

have a common denominator. $\frac{3\times5}{8\times5} = \frac{15}{40} \cdot \frac{3\times8}{5\times8} = \frac{24}{40}$. Now you will see that

$\frac{15}{40} \left(\frac{3}{8}\right)$ is less than, not greater than, $\frac{24}{40} \left(\frac{3}{5}\right)$.

D. $\frac{3}{4} > \frac{3}{5}$ (Yes. 0.75 is greater than 0.60.)

Domain: NF—Number and Operations—Fractions

25. **20°** Fifteen pieces of the pie were eaten, and three were remaining. That means that there were 18 equal pieces of pizza pie at the start. A pizza is a circle, and there are 360° in a circle. Therefore, 360 ÷ 18 = 20 *or* 18 × 20 = 360.

Domain: G—Geometry

26. **400 centimeters** Mia's car is 4 meters long. There are 100 centimeters in 1 meter. Multiply 4 by 100, which equals 400 centimeters.

Domain: MD—Measurement and Data

27. **(C)** All of the numbers in this set are factors of 72.

$$1 \times 72 = 72$$
$$2 \times 36 = 72$$
$$3 \times 24 = 72$$
$$4 \times 18 = 72$$
$$6 \times 12 = 72$$
$$8 \times 9 = 72$$

None of the other answer choices contain all of the factors of 72.

Domain: OA—Operations and Algebraic Thinking

28. **4,206** There were 2,316 board games and 1,890 video games donated. Add these numbers to find the total number of games that were donated: 2,316 + 1,890 = 4,206. Although the question says that there were 593 items of clothing donated, that is extra information that is not needed to answer the question.

Domain: NBT—Number and Operations in Base Ten

29. **(A)**, **(C)**, and **(D)**

A. $2,792 \div 4 \rightarrow 2,800 \div 4 = 700$ (YES)

B. $5,366 \div 9 \rightarrow 5,400 \div 9 = 600$ (NO)

C. $5,619 \div 8 \rightarrow 5,600 \div 8 = 700$ (YES)

D. $2,052 \div 3 \rightarrow 2,100 \div 3 = 700$ (YES)

Domain: NBT—Number and Operations in Base Ten

30. $1\frac{2}{4} + 2\frac{3}{4} = 3 + \frac{5}{4} = 3\frac{5}{4} = 4\frac{1}{4}$ Before the plus sign, there is 4 out of 4 boxes, or 1 whole, shaded in the first square and 2 out of 4 books, or one-half, shaded in the second square. This equals $1\frac{2}{4}$. After the plus sign, there is 4 out 4 boxes, or 1 whole, shaded in the first square, 4 out of 4 boxes, or 1 whole, shaded in the second square, and 3 out of 4 boxes, or three-fourths, shaded in the third square. This equals $2\frac{3}{4}$. Together, they add to $3\frac{5}{4}$, which can be simplified to $4\frac{1}{4}$.

Domain: NF—Number and Operations—Fractions

31. **(B)** The actual answer is 248 ÷ 3 = 82.$\overline{6}$. Choice B brings you to the closest estimate of this answer.

    Domain: NBT—Number and Operations in Base Ten

32. **(B)** The missing numbers at the top are **2** and **2**. The missing numbers at the bottom are **3**, **4**, **2**, and **4**. Your multiplication problem should look like:

$$22$$
$$856$$
$$\underline{\times \quad 4}$$
$$3424$$

    This is an example of traditional (standard) multiplication.

    Domain: NBT—Number and Operations in Base Ten

33. **(B)** To find out how many inches her plant grew over these three weeks, add together all of the growth measurements for each week.

$$1\frac{1}{2} + 3\frac{3}{4} + 2\frac{1}{4} = 1.5 + 3.75 + 2.25 = 7.5 = 7\frac{1}{2} \text{ inches}$$

    Domain: NF—Number and Operations—Fractions

34. **(C)** There are 60 minutes in 1 hour. There are also 30 minutes in 1 half hour.

$$60 + 60 + 60 + 30 = 210$$

    or

$$(60 \times 3) + 30 = 180 + 30 = 210$$

    Domain: MD—Measurement and Data

35. **(A)** and **(C)** are both correct. Manny needs to paint 4 walls. It will take $\frac{3}{5}$ gallon of paint to paint each of those 4 walls. Therefore, you can multiply 4 times $\frac{3}{5}$, which equals $\frac{12}{5}$. If you divide the numerator by the denominator, you can turn the fraction into a mixed number, $2\frac{2}{5}$. Another method of solving would be to add $\frac{3}{5}$ four times ($\frac{3}{5} + \frac{3}{5} + \frac{3}{5} + \frac{3}{5}$), which would equal $\frac{12}{5}$. Then,

12 ÷ 5 = 2 with 2 left over. Therefore, in the mixed number, the whole number is 2, the numerator of the fraction is 2, and the denominator of the fraction is 5.

The mixed number is $2\frac{2}{5}$.

Domain: NF—Number and Operations—Fractions

36. Your table should read as follows:

Less than $\frac{1}{2}$	Equal to $\frac{1}{2}$	Greater than $\frac{1}{2}$
$\frac{3}{8}$	$\frac{8}{16}$	$\frac{5}{8}$
$\frac{4}{12}$	$\frac{5}{10}$	$\frac{2}{3}$

When deciding if a fraction is "less than," "equal to," or "greater than" $\frac{1}{2}$, just look at the numerator. If the numerator is exactly half of the denominator, then the fraction is equal to $\frac{1}{2}$. If the numerator is less than half of the denominator, then the fraction is less than $\frac{1}{2}$. If the numerator is greater than half of the denominator, then the fraction is greater than $\frac{1}{2}$.

Domain: NF—Number and Operations—Fractions

37. The three rectangles that have an area of 24 are marked with Xs below.

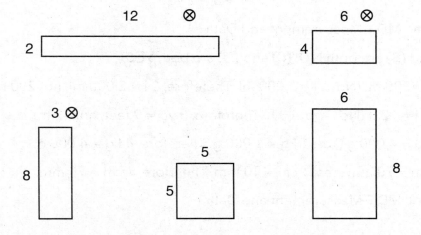

$$12 \times 2 = 24$$

$$4 \times 6 = 24$$

$$8 \times 3 = 24$$

$$5 \times 5 \neq 24 \text{ (It actually equals 25.)}$$

$$6 \times 8 \neq 24 \text{ (It actually equals 48.)}$$

Domain: MD—Measurement and Data

38. Your table should read as follows:

4 c	**32 fl oz**
10,000 lb	5 T
72 in	**6 ft**
7 yd	21 ft

There are 8 fluid ounces in 1 cup. Therefore:

$$4 \times 8 = 32 \text{ fl oz}$$

There are 2,000 lb in 1 ton. Therefore:

$$5 \times 2,000 = 10,000 \text{ lb}$$

There are 12 inches in 1 foot. Therefore:

$$72 \div 12 = 6 \text{ ft}$$

There are 3 feet in 1 yard. Therefore:

$$21 \div 3 = 7 \text{ yd}$$

Domain: MD—Measurement and Data

39. **(A)** and **(B)** are both **NO**. **(C)** and **(D)** are both **YES**.

   A. 2 l = 200 ml (No. 1 l = 1,000 ml. Therefore, 2 l = 2,000 ml, not 200 ml.)

   B. 3 yd = 12 ft (No. 1 yd = 3 ft. Therefore, 3 yd = 9 feet, not 12 ft.)

   C. 4 kg = 4,000 g (Yes. 1 kg = 1,000 g. Therefore, 4 kg = 4,000 g.)

   D. 7 cm = 70 mm (Yes. 1 cm = 10 mm. Therefore, 7 cm = 70 mm.)

Domain: MD—Measurement and Data

40. *b* represents the number of degrees in each part by which the circle is divided. *a* represents the number of equal parts into which the circle is divided. For example, if the circle is divided into 3 equal parts (meaning that $a = 3$), then each part is 120° (meaning that $b = 120°$). In other words, $360° \div 3 = 120°$.

    Domain: G—Geometry

41. **(B)** Angle *MAG* is an acute angle, meaning that it is between 1°−89°. An obtuse angle, choice A, is between 91°−179°. A straight angle, choice C, is a straight line, which is exactly 180°. A right angle, choice D, is exactly 90°.

    Domain: G—Geometry

42. **6 × 12 ≠ 73**. In the table, Hans recorded that $6 \times 12 = 73$. That is incorrect. 6×12 actually equals 72. All of the other facts in the table are correct.

    Domain: OA—Operations and Algebraic Thinking

43. Your completed area model and equation should read as follows:

	10	**+**	**7**	**=**	**17**

	1 5 3	6 3
9	− 9 0	− 6 3
	6 3	0

    This area model shows that $153 \div 9 = 17$.

    Domain: OA—Operations and Algebraic Thinking

Note: Questions 44 and 45 are both examples of how the questions on the Grade 4 Smarter Balanced Assessment could reach the 5th grade level.

44. Your completed area model and equation should read as follows:

	10	**+**	**5**	**=**	**15**

	2 4 0	8 0
16	− 1 6 0	− 8 0
	8 0	0

    This area model shows that $240 \div 16 = 15$.

    Domain: OA—Operations and Algebraic Thinking

45. **Part A:** Your equation should read: **270 ÷ 8 = h.** This results in **33 with a remainder of 6.** To put the remainder in fraction form, use the remainder, 6, as the numerator and the divisor, 8, as the denominator. The remainder in fraction form makes the final answer, $33\frac{6}{8}$ or $33\frac{3}{4}$. Since Mr. Santiago cannot buy three-quarters of a package, you need to round your answer up to the nearest whole number, meaning that Mr. Santiago must buy **34 packages of hot dog rolls**.

Part B: Your equation should read: **350 ÷ 8 = b.** This results in **43 with a remainder of 6.** To put the remainder in fraction form, use the remainder, 6, as the numerator and the divisor, 8, as the denominator. The remainder in fraction form makes the final answer, $43\frac{6}{8}$ or $43\frac{3}{4}$. Again, since Mr. Santiago cannot buy three-quarters of a package, you need to round your answer up to the nearest whole number, meaning that Mr. Santiago must buy **44 packages of hamburger rolls**.

Part C: Mr. Santiago will spend **$312** on rolls for the barbeque. To find this answer, first add the total number of packages of hot dog rolls and hamburger rolls.

$$34 + 44 = 78 \text{ packages total}$$

Then, multiply the total number of packages by the cost per package.

$$78 \text{ packages} \times \$4.00 \text{ per package} = \$312$$

Domain: OA—Operations and Algebraic Thinking

Performance Task, page 176

1. **Part A:** Your table should read as follows:

Item	Number of Boxes Needed
Cookies	2
Cupcakes	4
Eclairs	8
Tarts	24
Danish pastries	12

Part B: Your table should read as follows:

Item	Equations Used
Cookies	48 ÷ 24 = 2 or 2 × 24 = 48
Cupcakes	48 ÷ 12 = 4 or 4 × 12 = 48
Eclairs	48 ÷ 6 = 8 or 8 × 6 = 48
Tarts	48 ÷ 2 = 24 or 24 × 2 = 48
Danish pastries	48 ÷ 4 = 12 or 12 × 4 = 48

As you can see, to find the number of boxes needed for each item, you can either use division or multiplication equations. If you use division, you need to divide the number of each item that Stephanie makes each weekday, 48 items, by the amounts of each item that fit in one box. If you use multiplication, you need to figure out what number times the amount that fits in one box equals 48, the number of each item that Stephanie makes each weekday.

Part C: 50 boxes total To solve this part of the question, add together all of the number of boxes per item that you found in Part A.

$$2 + 4 + 8 + 24 + 12 = 50 \text{ boxes}$$

Part D: True, False, True Yes, the amount of eclairs made per day, 8, and the amount of tarts made per day, 24, are both multiples of 8. No, Danish pastries do not fill the most boxes. Tarts fill the most boxes. Yes, the number of boxes needed for each item is always an even number. All of the amounts (2, 4, 8, 24, and 12) are all even numbers.

2. **Part A: 5** trays are needed. Your completed workspace should match the following:

___5___ trays are needed.

V	V	V	V	V
V	V	V	C	C

C	C	C	C	C
C	C	RV	RV	RV

RV	RV	RV	PB	PB
PB	PB	PB	RS	RS

RS	RS	RS	RS	RS
RS	RS	RS	RS	RS

RS	RS	RS	RS	RS
RS				

In the first tray, 8 out of 10 spots should be filled with "**V**" to represent the fact that $\frac{8}{10}$ of a tray will be vanilla cupcakes. Then, the last 2 spots of the first tray and the first 7 spots of the second tray should be filled with "**C**" to represent the fact that $\frac{9}{10}$ of a tray will be chocolate cupcakes. Next, the last 3 spots of the second tray and the first 3 spots of the third tray should be filled with "**RV**" to represent the fact that $\frac{6}{10}$ of a tray will be red velvet cupcakes. Then, the next 5 spots of the third tray should be filled with "**PB**" to represent the fact that $\frac{5}{10}$ of a tray will be peanut butter cupcakes. Next, the last 2 spots of the third tray, all 10 spots of the fourth tray, and the first 6 spots of the fifth tray should be filled with "**RS**" to represent the fact that $\frac{9}{5}$ of a tray will be rainbow sprinkle cupcakes. Note, when both the numerator and the denominator of the fraction $\frac{9}{5}$ are multiplied by 2, the fraction becomes $\frac{18}{10}$. That is why 18 spots (2 + 10 + 6) are filled with "**RS**." Finally, add all of the fractions together to find the total number of trays needed.

$$\frac{8}{10} + \frac{9}{10} + \frac{6}{10} + \frac{5}{10} + \frac{18}{10} = \frac{46}{10} = 4\frac{6}{10}$$

Since $4\frac{6}{10}$ is a mixed number, you need to round up to the next whole number to find the answer. The next whole number is 5. Therefore, Stephanie will need 5 trays to display all of these cupcakes.

Part B: $\frac{4}{10}$ The fraction for each whole tray is $\frac{10}{10}$. We know from Part A that $\frac{6}{10}$ of the last tray is already filled. Therefore, in your equation, subtract $\frac{6}{10}$ from $\frac{10}{10}$ to find the correct answer.

$$\frac{10}{10} - \frac{6}{10} = \frac{4}{10}$$

Part C: Your response should read as follows:

There are more ____rainbow sprinkle____ cupcakes because ____the number____

of chocolate cupcakes, $\frac{9}{10}$, is less than the number of rainbow

sprinkle cupcakes, $\frac{18}{10}$.

3. **Part A: $115** From Question 2, you know that there are 46 cupcakes in the display. From the table at the start of the Performance Task, you know that cupcakes cost $2.50. Therefore, multiply these two numbers together to get the total cost for the cupcakes.

$$46 \times 2.50 = 115$$

The cupcake display for the birthday party will cost $115.

Part B: The total weekly order costs **$86.50**. The change received is **$13.50**. To find the total weekly order cost, multiply the number of each item by the cost of each item found in the table at the start of the performance task. Note that 1 dozen equals 12.

$$2 \text{ dozen cookies} = 24 \text{ cookies} \times \$0.75 \text{ per cookie} = \$18.00$$

$$12 \text{ eclairs} \times \$3.00 \text{ per eclair} = \$36.00$$

$$10 \text{ tarts} \times \$3.25 \text{ per tart} = \$32.50$$

Now, add all the amounts together to find the total.

$$\$18.00 + \$36.00 + \$32.50 = \$86.50$$

To find how much change the club would receive if they pay with a $100 bill, subtract the total weekly order cost from $100.

$$\$100 - \$86.50 = \$13.50$$

Note, when answering all of the Performance Task questions, it is very important that you correctly answer as many parts of the question as possible to achieve all of the points for that question. Below is a breakdown of each item from the Performance Task and how many points each section of the question is worth.

Question	Total Number of Points the Question Is Worth	Scoring Rubric
1A	5	Each correct answer (identifying the number of boxes needed for each of the 5 pastry items) is worth 1 point.
1B	5	Each correct answer (providing two equations for each pastry item) is worth 1 point.
1C	2	1 point is awarded for identifying the correct number of boxes. 1 point is awarded for correctly explaining how you reached that answer.
1D	3	1 point is awarded for identifying the first statement as true. 1 point is awarded for identifying the second statement as false. 1 point is awarded for identifying the third statement as true.
2A	3	2 points are awarded for creating the correct visual model. 1 point is awarded for providing the correct answer.
2B	2	1 point is awarded for providing the correct answer, or an equivalent of the correct answer. 1 point is awarded for providing a correct explanation with a correct equation.

Question	Total Number of Points the Question Is Worth	Scoring Rubric
2C	2	1 point is awarded for providing the correct answer (rainbow sprinkles). 1 point is awarded for providing the correct explanation (that $\frac{9}{10}$ is less than $\frac{18}{10}$).
3A	2	1 point is awarded for providing the correct answer. 1 point is awarded for providing the correct explanation.
3B	4	1 point is awarded for providing the correct answer for the total weekly order cost. 1 point is awarded for correctly explaining how you found the total weekly order cost. 1 point is awarded for providing the correct answer for how much change was received. 1 point is awarded for correctly explaining how you determined how much change was received.

Common Core Standards

English Language Arts Standards

Reading: Literature

Key Ideas and Details

CCSS.ELA-LITERACY.RL.4.1   Refer to details and examples in a text when explaining what the text says explicitly and when drawing inferences from the text.

CCSS.ELA-LITERACY.RL.4.2   Determine a theme of a story, drama, or poem from details in the text; summarize the text.

CCSS.ELA-LITERACY.RL.4.3   Describe in depth a character, setting, or event in a story or drama, drawing on specific details in the text (e.g., a character's thoughts, words, or actions).

Craft and Structure

CCSS.ELA-LITERACY.RL.4.4   Determine the meaning of words and phrases as they are used in a text, including those that allude to significant characters found in mythology (e.g., Herculean).

CCSS.ELA-LITERACY.RL.4.5   Explain major differences between poems, drama, and prose, and refer to the structural elements of poems (e.g., verse, rhythm, meter) and drama (e.g., casts of characters, settings, descriptions, dialogue, stage directions) when writing or speaking about a text.

CCSS.ELA-LITERACY.RL.4.6   Compare and contrast the point of view from which different stories are narrated, including the difference between first- and third-person narrations.

Integration of Knowledge and Ideas

CCSS.ELA-LITERACY.RL.4.7   Make connections between the text of a story or drama and a visual or oral presentation of the text, identifying where each version reflects specific descriptions and directions in the text.

CCSS.ELA-LITERACY.RL.4.8   (RL.4.8 not applicable to literature)

CCSS.ELA-LITERACY.RL.4.9   Compare and contrast the treatment of similar themes and topics (e.g., opposition of good and evil) and patterns of events (e.g., the quest) in stories, myths, and traditional literature from different cultures.

Range of Reading and Level of Text Complexity

CCSS.ELA-LITERACY.RL.4.10   By the end of the year, read and comprehend literature, including stories, dramas, and poetry, in the grades 4–5 text complexity band proficiently, with scaffolding as needed at the high end of the range.

Reading: Informational Text

Key Ideas and Details

CCSS.ELA-LITERACY.RI.4.1   Refer to details and examples in a text when explaining what the text says explicitly and when drawing inferences from the text.

CCSS.ELA-LITERACY.RI.4.2   Determine the main idea of a text and explain how it is supported by key details; summarize the text.

CCSS.ELA-LITERACY.RI.4.3   Explain events, procedures, ideas, or concepts in a historical, scientific, or technical text, including what happened and why, based on specific information in the text.

Craft and Structure

CCSS.ELA-LITERACY.RI.4.4   Determine the meaning of general academic and domain-specific words or phrases in a text relevant to a *grade 4 topic or subject area.*

CCSS.ELA-LITERACY.RI.4.5   Describe the overall structure (e.g., chronology, comparison, cause/effect, problem/solution) of events, ideas, concepts, or information in a text or part of a text.

CCSS.ELA-LITERACY.RI.4.6   Compare and contrast a firsthand and secondhand account of the same event or topic; describe the differences in focus and the information provided.

Integration of Knowledge and Ideas

CCSS.ELA-LITERACY.RI.4.7   Interpret information presented visually, orally, or quantitatively (e.g., in charts, graphs, diagrams, time lines, animations, or interactive elements on webpages) and explain how the information contributes to an understanding of the text in which it appears.

CCSS.ELA-LITERACY.RI.4.8   Explain how an author uses reasons and evidence to support particular points in a text.

CCSS.ELA-LITERACY.RI.4.9   Integrate information from two texts on the same topic in order to write or speak about the subject knowledgeably.

Range of Reading and Level of Text Complexity

CCSS.ELA-LITERACY.RI.4.10   By the end of year, read and comprehend informational texts, including history/social studies, science, and technical texts, in the grades 4–5 text complexity band proficiently, with scaffolding as needed at the high end of the range.

Reading Foundational Skills

Phonics and Word Recognition

CCSS.ELA-LITERACY.RF.4.3   Know and apply grade-level phonics and word analysis skills in decoding words.

> **CCSS.ELA-LITERACY.RF.4.3.A**
> Use combined knowledge of all letter-sound correspondences, syllabication patterns, and morphology (e.g., roots and affixes) to read accurately unfamiliar multisyllabic words in context and out of context.

Fluency

CCSS.ELA-LITERACY.RF.4.4   Read with sufficient accuracy and fluency to support comprehension.

> **CCSS.ELA-LITERACY.RF.4.4.A**
> Read grade-level text with purpose and understanding.

> **CCSS.ELA-LITERACY.RF.4.4.B**
> Read grade-level prose and poetry orally with accuracy, appropriate rate, and expression on successive readings.

> **CCSS.ELA-LITERACY.RF.4.4.C**
> Use context to confirm or self-correct word recognition and understanding, rereading as necessary.

Writing

Text Types and Purposes

CCSS.ELA-LITERACY.W.4.1   Write opinion pieces on topics or texts, supporting a point of view with reasons and information.

CCSS.ELA-LITERACY.W.4.1.A
Introduce a topic or text clearly, state an opinion, and create an organizational structure in which related ideas are grouped to support the writer's purpose.

CCSS.ELA-LITERACY.W.4.1.B
Provide reasons that are supported by facts and details.

CCSS.ELA-LITERACY.W.4.1.C
Link opinion and reasons using words and phrases (e.g., *for instance, in order to, in addition*).

CCSS.ELA-LITERACY.W.4.1.D
Provide a concluding statement or section related to the opinion presented.

CCSS.ELA-LITERACY.W.4.2   Write informative/explanatory texts to examine a topic and convey ideas and information clearly.

CCSS.ELA-LITERACY.W.4.2.A
Introduce a topic clearly and group related information in paragraphs and sections; include formatting (e.g., headings), illustrations, and multimedia when useful to aiding comprehension.

CCSS.ELA-LITERACY.W.4.2.B
Develop the topic with facts, definitions, concrete details, quotations, or other information and examples related to the topic.

CCSS.ELA-LITERACY.W.4.2.C
Link ideas within categories of information using words and phrases (e.g., *another, for example, also, because*).

CCSS.ELA-LITERACY.W.4.2.D
Use precise language and domain-specific vocabulary to inform about or explain the topic.

CCSS.ELA-LITERACY.W.4.2.E
Provide a concluding statement or section related to the information or explanation presented.

CCSS.ELA-LITERACY.W.4.3 Write narratives to develop real or imagined experiences or events using effective technique, descriptive details, and clear event sequences.

CCSS.ELA-LITERACY.W.4.3.A
Orient the reader by establishing a situation and introducing a narrator and/or characters; organize an event sequence that unfolds naturally.

CCSS.ELA-LITERACY.W.4.3.B
Use dialogue and description to develop experiences and events or show the responses of characters to situations.

CCSS.ELA-LITERACY.W.4.3.C
Use a variety of transitional words and phrases to manage the sequence of events.

CCSS.ELA-LITERACY.W.4.3.D
Use concrete words and phrases and sensory details to convey experiences and events precisely.

CCSS.ELA-LITERACY.W.4.3.E
Provide a conclusion that follows from the narrated experiences or events.

Production and Distribution of Writing

CCSS.ELA-LITERACY.W.4.4 Produce clear and coherent writing in which the development and organization are appropriate to task, purpose, and audience. (Grade-specific expectations for writing types are defined in standards 1–3 above.)

CCSS.ELA-LITERACY.W.4.5 With guidance and support from peers and adults, develop and strengthen writing as needed by planning, revising, and editing. (Editing for conventions should demonstrate command of Language Standards 1–3 up to and including grade 4 here.)

CCSS.ELA-LITERACY.W.4.6 With some guidance and support from adults, use technology, including the Internet, to produce and publish writing as well as to interact and collaborate with others; demonstrate sufficient command of keyboarding skills to type a minimum of one page in a single sitting.

Research to Build and Present Knowledge

CCSS.ELA-LITERACY.W.4.7   Conduct short research projects that build knowledge through investigation of different aspects of a topic.

CCSS.ELA-LITERACY.W.4.8   Recall relevant information from experiences or gather relevant information from print and digital sources; take notes and categorize information, and provide a list of sources.

CCSS.ELA-LITERACY.W.4.9   Draw evidence from literary or informational texts to support analysis, reflection, and research.

CCSS.ELA-LITERACY.W.4.9.A
Apply *grade 4 Reading standards* to literature (e.g., "Describe in depth a character, setting, or event in a story or drama, drawing on specific details in the text [e.g., a character's thoughts, words, or actions].").

CCSS.ELA-LITERACY.W.4.9.B
Apply *grade 4 Reading standards* to informational texts (e.g., "Explain how an author uses reasons and evidence to support particular points in a text").

Range of Writing

CCSS.ELA-LITERACY.W.4.10   Write routinely over extended time frames (time for research, reflection, and revision) and shorter time frames (a single sitting or a day or two) for a range of discipline-specific tasks, purposes, and audiences.

Speaking and Listening

Comprehension and Collaboration

CCSS.ELA-LITERACY.SL.4.1   Engage effectively in a range of collaborative discussions (one-on-one, in groups, and teacher-led) with diverse partners on grade 4 topics and texts, building on others' ideas and expressing their own clearly.

CCSS.ELA-LITERACY.SL.4.1.A
Come to discussions prepared, having read or studied required material; explicitly draw on that preparation and other information known about the topic to explore ideas under discussion.

CCSS.ELA-LITERACY.SL.4.1.B
Follow agreed-upon rules for discussions and carry out assigned roles.

CCSS.ELA-LITERACY.SL.4.1.C
Pose and respond to specific questions to clarify or follow up on information, and make comments that contribute to the discussion and link to the remarks of others.

CCSS.ELA-LITERACY.SL.4.1.D
Review the key ideas expressed and explain their own ideas and understanding in light of the discussion.

CCSS.ELA-LITERACY.SL.4.2   Paraphrase portions of a text read aloud or information presented in diverse media and formats, including visually, quantitatively, and orally.

CCSS.ELA-LITERACY.SL.4.3   Identify the reasons and evidence a speaker provides to support particular points.

Presentation of Knowledge and Ideas

CCSS.ELA-LITERACY.SL.4.4   Report on a topic or text, tell a story, or recount an experience in an organized manner, using appropriate facts and relevant, descriptive details to support main ideas or themes; speak clearly at an understandable pace.

CCSS.ELA-LITERACY.SL.4.5   Add audio recordings and visual displays to presentations when appropriate to enhance the development of main ideas or themes.

CCSS.ELA-LITERACY.SL.4.6   Differentiate between contexts that call for formal English (e.g., presenting ideas) and situations where informal discourse is appropriate (e.g., small-group discussion); use formal English when appropriate to task and situation. (See grade 4 Language standards 1 here for specific expectations.)

Language

Conventions of Standard English

CCSS.ELA-LITERACY.L.4.1   Demonstrate command of the conventions of standard English grammar and usage when writing or speaking.

CCSS.ELA-LITERACY.L.4.1.A
Use relative pronouns (who, whose, whom, which, that) and relative adverbs (where, when, why).

CCSS.ELA-LITERACY.L.4.1.B
Form and use the progressive (e.g., I was walking; I am walking; I will be walking) verb tenses.

CCSS.ELA-LITERACY.L.4.1.C
Use modal auxiliaries (e.g., can, may, must) to convey various conditions.

CCSS.ELA-LITERACY.L.4.1.D
Order adjectives within sentences according to conventional patterns (e.g., *a small red bag* rather than *a red small bag*).

CCSS.ELA-LITERACY.L.4.1.E

Form and use prepositional phrases.

CCSS.ELA-LITERACY.L.4.1.F

Produce complete sentences, recognizing and correcting inappropriate fragments and run-ons.

CCSS.ELA-LITERACY.L.4.1.G

Correctly use frequently confused words (e.g., to, too, two; there, their).

CCSS.ELA-LITERACY.L.4.2 Demonstrate command of the conventions of standard English capitalization, punctuation, and spelling when writing.

CCSS.ELA-LITERACY.L.4.2.A

Use correct capitalization.

CCSS.ELA-LITERACY.L.4.2.B

Use commas and quotation marks to mark direct speech and quotations from a text.

CCSS.ELA-LITERACY.L.4.2.C

Use a comma before a coordinating conjunction in a compound sentence.

CCSS.ELA-LITERACY.L.4.2.D

Spell grade-appropriate words correctly, consulting references as needed.

Knowledge of Language

CCSS.ELA-LITERACY.L.4.3 Use knowledge of language and its conventions when writing, speaking, reading, or listening.

CCSS.ELA-LITERACY.L.4.3.A

Choose words and phrases to convey ideas precisely.

CCSS.ELA-LITERACY.L.4.3.B

Choose punctuation for effect.

CCSS.ELA-LITERACY.L.4.3.C

Differentiate between contexts that call for formal English (e.g., presenting ideas) and situations where informal discourse is appropriate (e.g., small-group discussion).

Vocabulary Acquisition and Use

CCSS.ELA-LITERACY.L.4.4 Determine or clarify the meaning of unknown and multiple-meaning words and phrases based on grade 4 reading and content, choosing flexibly from a range of strategies.

CCSS.ELA-LITERACY.L.4.4.A
Use context (e.g., definitions, examples, or restatements in text) as a clue to the meaning of a word or phrase.

CCSS.ELA-LITERACY.L.4.4.B
Use common, grade-appropriate Greek and Latin affixes and roots as clues to the meaning of a word (e.g., telegraph, photograph, autograph).

CCSS.ELA-LITERACY.L.4.4.C
Consult reference materials (e.g., dictionaries, glossaries, thesauruses), both print and digital, to find the pronunciation and determine or clarify the precise meaning of key words and phrases.

CCSS.ELA-LITERACY.L.4.5 Demonstrate understanding of figurative language, word relationships, and nuances in word meanings.

CCSS.ELA-LITERACY.L.4.5.A
Explain the meaning of simple similes and metaphors (e.g., as pretty as a picture) in context.

CCSS.ELA-LITERACY.L.4.5.B
Recognize and explain the meaning of common idioms, adages, and proverbs.

CCSS.ELA-LITERACY.L.4.5.C
Demonstrate understanding of words by relating them to their opposites (antonyms) and to words with similar but not identical meanings (synonyms).

CCSS.ELA-LITERACY.L.4.6 Acquire and use accurately grade-appropriate general academic and domain-specific words and phrases, including those that signal precise actions, emotions, or states of being (e.g., quizzed, whined, stammered) and that are basic to a particular topic (e.g., wildlife, conservation, and endangered when discussing animal preservation).

Math Standards

Operations and Algebraic Thinking

Use the Four Operations with Whole Numbers to Solve Problems

CCSS.MATH.CONTENT.4.OA.A.1   Interpret a multiplication equation as a comparison, e.g., interpret $35 = 5 \times 7$ as a statement that 35 is 5 times as many as 7 and 7 times as many as 5. Represent verbal statements of multiplicative comparisons as multiplication equations.

CCSS.MATH.CONTENT.4.OA.A.2   Multiply or divide to solve word problems involving multiplicative comparison, e.g., by using drawings and equations with a symbol for the unknown number to represent the problem, distinguishing multiplicative comparison from additive comparison.

CCSS.MATH.CONTENT.4.OA.A.3   Solve multistep word problems posed with whole numbers and having whole-number answers using the four operations, including problems in which remainders must be interpreted. Represent these problems using equations with a letter standing for the unknown quantity. Assess the reasonableness of answers using mental computation and estimation strategies including rounding.

Gain Familiarity with Factors and Multiples

CCSS.MATH.CONTENT.4.OA.B.4   Find all factor pairs for a whole number in the range 1–100. Recognize that a whole number is a multiple of each of its factors. Determine whether a given whole number in the range 1–100 is a multiple of a given one-digit number. Determine whether a given whole number in the range 1–100 is prime or composite.

Generate and Analyze Patterns

CCSS.MATH.CONTENT.4.OA.C.5   Generate a number or shape pattern that follows a given rule. Identify apparent features of the pattern that were not explicit in the rule itself. *For example, given the rule "Add 3" and the starting number 1, generate terms in the resulting sequence and observe that the terms appear to alternate between odd and even numbers. Explain informally why the numbers will continue to alternate in this way.*

Number and Operations in Base 10

Generalize Place Value Understanding for Multi-Digit Whole Numbers

CCSS.MATH.CONTENT.4.NBT.A.1 Recognize that in a multi-digit whole number, a digit in one place represents ten times what it represents in the place to its right. *For example, recognize that 700 ÷ 70 = 10 by applying concepts of place value and division.*

CCSS.MATH.CONTENT.4.NBT.A.2 Read and write multi-digit whole numbers using base-ten numerals, number names, and expanded form. Compare two multi-digit numbers based on meanings of the digits in each place, using >, =, and < symbols to record the results of comparisons.

CCSS.MATH.CONTENT.4.NBT.A.3 Use place value understanding to round multi-digit whole numbers to any place.

Use Place Value Understanding and Properties of Operations to Perform Multi-Digit Arithmetic

CCSS.MATH.CONTENT.4.NBT.B.4 Fluently add and subtract multi-digit whole numbers using the standard algorithm.

CCSS.MATH.CONTENT.4.NBT.B.5 Multiply a whole number of up to four digits by a one-digit whole number, and multiply two two-digit numbers, using strategies based on place value and the properties of operations. Illustrate and explain the calculation by using equations, rectangular arrays, and/or area models.

CCSS.MATH.CONTENT.4.NBT.B.6 Find whole-number quotients and remainders with up to four-digit dividends and one-digit divisors, using strategies based on place value, the properties of operations, and/or the relationship between multiplication and division. Illustrate and explain the calculation by using equations, rectangular arrays, and/or area models.

Number and Operations—Fractions

Extend Understanding of Fraction Equivalence and Ordering

CCSS.MATH.CONTENT.4.NF.A.1 Explain why a fraction a/b is equivalent to a fraction $(n \times a)/(n \times b)$ by using visual fraction models, with attention to how the number and size of the parts differ even though the two fractions themselves are the same size. Use this principle to recognize and generate equivalent fractions.

CCSS.MATH.CONTENT.4.NF.A.2 Compare two fractions with different numerators and different denominators, e.g., by creating common denominators or numerators, or by comparing to a benchmark fraction such as 1/2. Recognize that comparisons are valid only when the two fractions refer to the same whole. Record the results of comparisons with symbols >, =, or <, and justify the conclusions, e.g., by using a visual fraction model.

Build Fractions from Unit Fractions

CCSS.MATH.CONTENT.4.NF.B.3 Understand a fraction a/b with $a > 1$ as a sum of fractions $1/b$.

CCSS.MATH.CONTENT.4.NF.B.3.A
Understand addition and subtraction of fractions as joining and separating parts referring to the same whole.

CCSS.MATH.CONTENT.4.NF.B.3.B
Decompose a fraction into a sum of fractions with the same denominator in more than one way, recording each decomposition by an equation. Justify decompositions, e.g., by using a visual fraction model. *Examples: 3/8 = 1/8 + 1/8 + 1/8 ; 3/8 = 1/8 + 2/8 ; 2 1/8 = 1 + 1 + 1/8 = 8/8 + 8/8 + 1/8.*

CCSS.MATH.CONTENT.4.NF.B.3.C
Add and subtract mixed numbers with like denominators, e.g., by replacing each mixed number with an equivalent fraction, and/or by using properties of operations and the relationship between addition and subtraction.

CCSS.MATH.CONTENT.4.NF.B.3.D
Solve word problems involving addition and subtraction of fractions referring to the same whole and having like denominators, e.g., by using visual fraction models and equations to represent the problem.

CCSS.MATH.CONTENT.4.NF.B.4 Apply and extend previous understandings of multiplication to multiply a fraction by a whole number.

CCSS.MATH.CONTENT.4.NF.B.4.A
Understand a fraction a/b as a multiple of $1/b$. *For example, use a visual fraction model to represent 5/4 as the product 5 × (1/4), recording the conclusion by the equation 5/4 = 5 × (1/4).*

CCSS.MATH.CONTENT.4.NF.B.4.B
Understand a multiple of a/b as a multiple of $1/b$, and use this understanding to multiply a fraction by a whole number. *For example, use a visual fraction model to express 3 × (2/5) as 6 × (1/5), recognizing this product as 6/5. (In general, n × (a/b) = (n × a)/b.)*

CCSS.MATH.CONTENT.4.NF.B.4.C
Solve word problems involving multiplication of a fraction by a whole number, e.g., by using visual fraction models and equations to represent the problem. *For example, if each person at a party will eat 3/8 of a pound of roast beef, and there will be 5 people at the party, how many pounds of roast beef will be needed? Between what two whole numbers does your answer lie?*

Understand Decimal Notation for Fractions, and Compare Decimal Fractions

CCSS.MATH.CONTENT.4.NF.C.5 Express a fraction with denominator 10 as an equivalent fraction with denominator 100, and use this technique to add two fractions with respective denominators 10 and 100^2. *For example, express 3/10 as 30/100, and add 3/10 + 4/100 = 34/100.*

CCSS.MATH.CONTENT.4.NF.C.6 Use decimal notation for fractions with denominators 10 or 100. *For example, rewrite 0.62 as 62/100; describe a length as 0.62 meters; locate 0.62 on a number line diagram.*

CCSS.MATH.CONTENT.4.NF.C.7 Compare two decimals to hundredths by reasoning about their size. Recognize that comparisons are valid only when the two decimals refer to the same whole. Record the results of comparisons with the symbols >, =, or <, and justify the conclusions, e.g., by using a visual model.

Measurement and Data

Solve Problems Involving Measurement and Conversion of Measurements

CCSS.MATH.CONTENT.4.MD.A.1 Know relative sizes of measurement units within one system of units including km, m, cm; kg, g; lb, oz.; l, ml; hr, min, sec. Within a single system of measurement, express measurements in a larger unit in terms of a smaller unit. Record measurement equivalents in a two-column table. *For example, know that 1 ft is 12 times as long as 1 in. Express the length of a 4 ft snake as 48 in. Generate a conversion table for feet and inches listing the number pairs (1, 12), (2, 24), (3, 36), ...*

CCSS.MATH.CONTENT.4.MD.A.2 Use the four operations to solve word problems involving distances, intervals of time, liquid volumes, masses of objects, and money, including problems involving simple fractions or decimals, and problems that require expressing measurements given in a larger unit in terms of a smaller unit. Represent measurement quantities using diagrams such as number line diagrams that feature a measurement scale.

CCSS.MATH.CONTENT.4.MD.A.3 Apply the area and perimeter formulas for rectangles in real world and mathematical problems. *For example, find the width of a rectangular room given the area of the flooring and the length, by viewing the area formula as a multiplication equation with an unknown factor.*

Represent and Interpret Data

CCSS.MATH.CONTENT.4.MD.B.4 Make a line plot to display a data set of measurements in fractions of a unit (1/2, 1/4, 1/8). Solve problems involving addition and subtraction of fractions by using information presented in line plots. *For example, from a line plot find and interpret the difference in length between the longest and shortest specimens in an insect collection.*

Geometric Measurement: Understand Concepts of Angle and Measure Angles

CCSS.MATH.CONTENT.4.MD.C.5 Recognize angles as geometric shapes that are formed wherever two rays share a common endpoint, and understand concepts of angle measurement:

> **CCSS.MATH.CONTENT.4.MD.C.5.A**
> An angle is measured with reference to a circle with its center at the common endpoint of the rays, by considering the fraction of the circular arc between the points where the two rays intersect the circle. An angle that turns through 1/360 of a circle is called a "one-degree angle," and can be used to measure angles.

> **CCSS.MATH.CONTENT.4.MD.C.5.B**
> An angle that turns through n one-degree angles is said to have an angle measure of n degrees.

CCSS.MATH.CONTENT.4.MD.C.6 Measure angles in whole-number degrees using a protractor. Sketch angles of specified measure.

CCSS.MATH.CONTENT.4.MD.C.7 Recognize angle measure as additive. When an angle is decomposed into non-overlapping parts, the angle measure of the whole is the sum of the angle measures of the parts. Solve addition and subtraction problems to find unknown angles on a diagram in real world and mathematical problems, e.g., by using an equation with a symbol for the unknown angle measure.

Geometry

Draw and Identify Lines and Angles, and Classify Shapes by Properties of Their Lines and Angles

CCSS.MATH.CONTENT.4.G.A.1 Draw points, lines, line segments, rays, angles (right, acute, obtuse), and perpendicular and parallel lines. Identify these in two-dimensional figures.

CCSS.MATH.CONTENT.4.G.A.2 Classify two-dimensional figures based on the presence or absence of parallel or perpendicular lines, or the presence or absence of angles of a specified size. Recognize right triangles as a category, and identify right triangles.

CCSS.MATH.CONTENT.4.G.A.3 Recognize a line of symmetry for a two-dimensional figure as a line across the figure such that the figure can be folded along the line into matching parts. Identify line-symmetric figures and draw lines of symmetry.

Standards for Mathematical Practice

Note: All information in this Appendix sourced from official Common Core website *http://www.corestandards.org/*.

The Standards for Mathematical Practice describe varieties of expertise that mathematics educators at all levels should seek to develop in their students. These practices rest on important "processes and proficiencies" with longstanding importance in mathematics education. The first of these are the NCTM process standards of problem solving, reasoning and proof, communication, representation, and connections. The second are the strands of mathematical proficiency specified in the National Research Council's report *Adding It Up*: adaptive reasoning, strategic competence, conceptual understanding (comprehension of mathematical concepts, operations, and relations), procedural fluency (skill in carrying out procedures flexibly, accurately, efficiently, and appropriately), and productive disposition (habitual inclination to see mathematics as sensible, useful, and worthwhile, coupled with a belief in diligence and one's own efficacy).

The Standards for Mathematical Practices

1. **CCSS.MATH.PRACTICE.MP1—Make sense of problems and persevere in solving them.**

   Mathematically proficient students start by explaining to themselves the meaning of a problem and looking for entry points to its solution. They analyze givens, constraints, relationships, and goals. They make conjectures about the form and meaning of the solution and plan a solution pathway rather than simply jumping into a solution attempt. They consider analogous problems, and try special cases and simpler forms of the original problem in order to gain insight into its solution. They monitor and evaluate their progress and change course if necessary. Older students might, depending on the context of the problem, transform algebraic expressions or change the viewing window on their graphing calculator to get the information they need. Mathematically proficient students can explain correspondences between equations, verbal descriptions, tables, and graphs or draw diagrams of important features and relationships, graph data, and search for regularity or trends. Younger students might rely on using concrete objects or pictures to help conceptualize and solve a problem. Mathematically proficient students check their answers to problems using a different method, and they continually ask themselves, "Does this make sense?" They can understand the approaches of others to solving complex problems and identify correspondences between different approaches.

2. **CCSS.MATH.PRACTICE.MP2—Reason abstractly and quantitatively.**

Mathematically proficient students make sense of quantities and their relationships in problem situations. They bring two complementary abilities to bear on problems involving quantitative relationships: the ability to *decontextualize*—to abstract a given situation and represent it symbolically and manipulate the representing symbols as if they have a life of their own, without necessarily attending to their referents—and the ability to *contextualize*, to pause as needed during the manipulation process in order to probe into the referents for the symbols involved. Quantitative reasoning entails habits of creating a coherent representation of the problem at hand; considering the units involved; attending to the meaning of quantities, not just how to compute them; and knowing and flexibly using different properties of operations and objects.

3. **CCSS.MATH.PRACTICE.MP3—Construct viable arguments and critique the reasoning of others.**

Mathematically proficient students understand and use stated assumptions, definitions, and previously established results in constructing arguments. They make conjectures and build a logical progression of statements to explore the truth of their conjectures. They are able to analyze situations by breaking them into cases, and can recognize and use counterexamples. They justify their conclusions, communicate them to others, and respond to the arguments of others. They reason inductively about data, making plausible arguments that take into account the context from which the data arose. Mathematically proficient students are also able to compare the effectiveness of two plausible arguments, distinguish correct logic or reasoning from that which is flawed, and—if there is a flaw in an argument—explain what it is. Elementary students can construct arguments using concrete referents such as objects, drawings, diagrams, and actions. Such arguments can make sense and be correct, even though they are not generalized or made formal until later grades. Later, students learn to determine domains to which an argument applies. Students at all grades can listen or read the arguments of others, decide whether they make sense, and ask useful questions to clarify or improve the arguments.

4. **CCSS.MATH.PRACTICE.MP4—Model with mathematics.**

Mathematically proficient students can apply the mathematics they know to solve problems arising in everyday life, society, and the workplace. In early grades, this might be as simple as writing an addition equation to describe a situation. In middle grades, a student might apply proportional reasoning to plan a school event or analyze a problem in the community. By high school, a student might use geometry to solve a design problem or use a function to describe how one quantity of interest depends on another. Mathematically proficient students who can apply what they know are comfortable making assumptions and approximations to simplify a complicated situation, realizing that these may need revision later. They are able to identify important quantities in a practical situation and map their relationships using such tools as diagrams, two-way tables, graphs, flowcharts, and formulas. They can analyze those relationships mathematically to draw conclusions. They routinely interpret their mathematical results in the context of the situation and reflect on whether the results make sense, possibly improving the model if it has not served its purpose.

5. **CCSS.MATH.PRACTICE.MP5—Use appropriate tools strategically.**

Mathematically proficient students consider the available tools when solving a mathematical problem. These tools might include pencil and paper, concrete models, a ruler, a protractor, a calculator, a spreadsheet, a computer algebra system, a statistical package, or dynamic geometry software. Proficient students are sufficiently familiar with tools appropriate for their grade or course to make sound decisions about when each of these tools might be helpful, recognizing both the insight to be gained and their limitations. For example, mathematically proficient high school students analyze graphs of functions and solutions generated using a graphing calculator. They detect possible errors by strategically using estimation and other mathematical knowledge. When making mathematical models, they know that technology can enable them to visualize the results of varying assumptions, explore consequences, and compare predictions with data. Mathematically proficient students at various grade levels are able to identify relevant external mathematical resources, such as digital content located on a website, and use them to pose or solve problems. They are able to use technological tools to explore and deepen their understanding of concepts.

6. **CCSS.MATH.PRACTICE.MP6—Attend to precision.**

   Mathematically proficient students try to communicate precisely to others. They try to use clear definitions in discussion with others and in their own reasoning. They state the meaning of the symbols they choose, including using the equal sign consistently and appropriately. They are careful about specifying units of measure, and labeling axes to clarify the correspondence with quantities in a problem. They calculate accurately and efficiently and express numerical answers with a degree of precision appropriate for the problem context. In the elementary grades, students give carefully formulated explanations to each other. By the time they reach high school they have learned to examine claims and make explicit use of definitions.

7. **CCSS.MATH.PRACTICE.MP7—Look for and make use of structure.**

   Mathematically proficient students look closely to discern a pattern or structure. Young students, for example, might notice that three and seven more is the same amount as seven and three more, or they may sort a collection of shapes according to how many sides the shapes have. Later, students will see 7×8 equals the well remembered $7 \times 5 + 7 \times 3$, in preparation for learning about the distributive property. In the expression $x^2 + 9x + 14$, older students can see the 14 as 2×7 and the 9 as $2 + 7$. They recognize the significance of an existing line in a geometric figure and can use the strategy of drawing an auxiliary line for solving problems. They also can step back for an overview and shift perspective. They can see complicated things, such as some algebraic expressions, as single objects or as being composed of several objects. For example, they can see $5 - 3(x - y)^2$ as 5 minus a positive number times a square and use that to realize that its value cannot be more than 5 for any real numbers x and y.

8. **CCSS.MATH.PRACTICE.MP8—Look for and express regularity in repeated reasoning.**

   Mathematically proficient students notice if calculations are repeated, and look both for general methods and for shortcuts. Upper elementary students might notice when dividing 25 by 11 that they are repeating the same calculations over and over again, and conclude they have a repeating decimal. By paying attention to the calculation of slope as they repeatedly check whether points are on the line through (1, 2) with slope 3, middle school students might abstract the equation $(y - 2)/(x - 1) = 3$. Noticing the regularity in the way terms cancel when expanding $(x - 1)(x + 1)$, $(x - 1)(x^2 + x + 1)$, and $(x - 1)$ $(x^3 + x^2 + x + 1)$ might lead them to the general formula for the sum of a geometric series. As they work to solve a problem, mathematically proficient students maintain oversight of the process, while attending to the details. They continually evaluate the reasonableness of their intermediate results.

Connecting the Standards for Mathematical Practice to the Standards for Mathematical Content

The Standards for Mathematical Practice describe ways in which developing student practitioners of the discipline of mathematics increasingly ought to engage with the subject matter as they grow in mathematical maturity and expertise throughout the elementary, middle, and high school years. Designers of curricula, assessments, and professional development should all attend to the need to connect the mathematical practices to mathematical content in mathematics instruction.

The Standards for Mathematical Content are a balanced combination of procedure and understanding. Expectations that begin with the word "understand" are often especially good opportunities to connect the practices to the content. Students who lack understanding of a topic may rely on procedures too heavily. Without a flexible base from which to work, they may be less likely to consider analogous problems, represent problems coherently, justify conclusions, apply the mathematics to practical situations, use technology mindfully to work with the mathematics, explain the mathematics accurately to other students, step back for an overview, or deviate from a known procedure to find a shortcut. In short, a lack of understanding effectively prevents a student from engaging in the mathematical practices.

In this respect, those content standards that set an expectation of understanding are potential "points of intersection" between the Standards for Mathematical Content and the Standards for Mathematical Practice. These points of intersection are intended to be weighted toward central and generative concepts in the school mathematics curriculum that most merit the time, resources, innovative energies, and focus necessary to qualitatively improve the curriculum, instruction, assessment, professional development, and student achievement in mathematics.

Index

BARRON'S COMMON CORE SUCCESS

Barron's Educational Series

Barron's *Common Core Success* series offers help to students with an in-depth review of a full year's curriculum. Authored by seasoned educators who have successfully implemented Common Core in their own classrooms, these books are specifically designed to mirror the way teachers *actually* teach Math and English Language Arts (ELA) in the classroom, and include:

- "Ace It Time" checklists that guide students through the problem-solving process
- Units divided into thematic lessons and designed for self-guided study
- "Stop and Think" review sections that ensure students grasp concepts as they go along

These colorful, engaging workbooks present all the information children need to succeed throughout the school year and beyond.

Each book: Paperback, 8 3/8" x 10 7/8"
$12.99, *Can$15.50*

GRADE 4 **MATH**
978-1-4380-0676-5

GRADE 4 **ENGLISH LANGUAGE ARTS**
978-1-4380-0675-8

Also Available....

Covers Both
ELA & Math

CORE FOCUS

**GRADE 4
TEST PRACTICE
FOR COMMON CORE**

Help students practice and prepare for the all-important assessment tests at the end of the school year. Every turn of the page provides a new standard with hundreds of practice questions; an easy-to-follow, side-by-side layout that lets students conquer one standard at a time; student-friendly worksheets to reinforce what they're learning in the classroom; and more. It's an excellent resource for parents and teachers as they help students meet and exceed grade level expectations.

Paperback, 8 3/8" x 10 7/8", 978-1-4380-0515-7
$14.99, *Can$16.99*

Available at your local
book store or visit
www.barronseduc.com

Barron's Educational Series, Inc.
250 Wireless Blvd.
Hauppauge, N.Y. 11788
Order toll-free: 1-800-645-3476

Prices subject to change without notice.

In Canada:
Georgetown Book Warehouse
34 Armstrong Ave.
Georgetown, Ontario L7G 4R9
Canadian orders: 1-800-247-7160

(#309a) R6/16

PREPARE STUDENTS FOR SUCCESS

Let's Prepare for the PARCC . . . Tests

FULLY ALIGNED WITH NEW STATE STANDARDS

This series of books introduces students to the PARCC assessment administered across the country. It offers comprehensive subject reviews and practice tests designed to familiarize students with the PARCC grade level test and prepares them to do their best on test day.

Each of these books feature:

- An explanation and overview of the test, including the computerized format of the exams
- Two full-length practice tests with answers and explanations
- Practice exercises that cover the different types of PARCC questions
- Helpful test-taking tips and preparation techniques throughout
- Tactics to help students answer the ELA questions
- Strategies to help students navigate different math domains, including the number system, expression and equations, statistics and probability, geometry, and more

Students will find everything they need in order to prepare—and succeed— on the PARCC tests.

Let's Prepare for the PARCC Grade 4 ELA/Literacy Test
ISBN 978-1-4380-0813-4

Let's Prepare for the PARCC Grade 4 Math Test
ISBN 978-1-4380-0814-1

Each book: Paperback, 7 13/16" x 10", $12.99, *Can$15.50*

Smarter Balanced Books

This series of books introduces students to the *Smarter Balanced Assessment Consortium (SBAC)*, a series of next-generation assessment tests based on the Common Core Standards. These fair and reliable standards prepare students for 21st Century learning, including the use of computers on test day. These books feature two full-length practice tests (one in ELA and one in Math); an overview of the tests, including the computerized format of the exams; all questions thoroughly answered and explained; practice exercises that cover the different types of SBAC questions; test-taking tips and strategies; and more. It's the perfect way to help students reach their highest potential on the grade-specific SBAC tests.

Smarter Balanced Grade 4   ISBN 978-1-4380-0922-3
Paperback, 7 13/16" x 10", $14.99, *Can$17.99*

Available at your local book store
or visit **www.barronseduc.com**

Barron's Educational Series, Inc.
250 Wireless Blvd.
Hauppauge, NY 11788
Order toll-free: 1-800-645-3476
Prices subject to change without notice.

In Canada: Georgetown Book Warehouse
34 Armstrong Ave.
Georgetown, Ontario L7G 4R9
Canadian orders: 1-800-247-7160

(#311a) R9/16

ACTION . . . ADVENTURE . . . AND SCIENCE!

Everyday Science

66 experiments that explain the small and big things all around us

Eduardo Banqueri, Josep Mª Barres, Laia Barres, and Octavi López Coronado; Illustrations by Roger Zanni

You don't need a laboratory full of expensive equipment to be a super cool science sleuth! With help from **Everyday Science**, budding scientists will gain practical knowledge while learning how to:

- Build a time machine
- Guess tomorrow's weather
- Generate salty stalactites
- Make a rainbow disappear, and more.

Amaze your family and friends with these original, fun, and surprising experiments that will help you discover the many fun ways that science can be applied to the real world. (Ages 8 and up)

PUB. DATE: SEPTEMBER
Paperback, 9 1/4" x 11", ISBN 978-1-4380-0862-2
$14.99, Can$17.99

S.T.E.M. Squad

Aaron Rosenberg

When a rich patron funds a pilot program to get children excited by S.T.E.M. subjects, five students are hand-picked for the project. Some of the students are excited to be there, and some of them couldn't care less. But as problems arise, it's the S.T.E.M. Squad to the rescue! Kids will enjoy watching these ordinary kids rise to any challenge as the S.T.E.M. Squad teams up with top-notch scientists, engineers, mathematicians, geologists, and others, and learns that applied science can be fun! (Ages 9+)

PUB. DATE: DECEMBER
Each book: Paperback, 5 1/4" x 7 9/16"
$7.99, Can$9.50

Flood: Race Against Time
ISBN 978-1-4380-0805-9

Blackout: Danger in the Dark
ISBN 978-1-4380-0921-6

Available at your local book store or visit **www.barronseduc.com**

Barron's Educational Series, Inc.
250 Wireless Blvd.
Hauppauge, NY 11788
Order toll-free: 1-800-645-3476

In Canada: Georgetown Book Warehouse
34 Armstrong Ave.
Georgetown, Ont. L7G 4R9
Canadian orders: 1-800-247-7160

Prices subject to change without notice.

(#308) R5/16

Learn all about our government!

Presidential Elections

And Other Cool Facts, 4th Edition

"Presidential Elections and Other Cool Facts by Syl Sobel, J.D., is both interesting and easy to understand. Line drawings carry the reader through the engaging and informative text. For a simple, straightforward explanation of the election process, this book is hard to beat."

—*The Boston Herald*

Paperback, 978-1-4380-0691-8, $6.99, *Can$8.50*

The U. S. Constitution and You, 2nd Edition

"A difficult subject becomes easy for inquisitive young minds to read and understand in this book full of information about our nation ... Recommended."

—*Library Talk*

Paperback, 978-0-7641-4794-4, $6.99, *Can$7.99*

How the U.S. Government Works, 2nd Edition

This book explains the federal system as it works today, more than two hundred years after the framers of the Constitution brought it into existence. Covered here are the Legislative body, composed of the Senate and House of Representatives, the Executive branch, headed by the President and consisting of Cabinet members, and the Judicial branch, headed by the U.S. Supreme Court, and extending to federal courts throughout the nation.
Paperback, 978-0-7641-4792-0, $6.99, *Can$7.99*

The Bill of Rights

In 1787, after the U.S. Constitution had been ratified, many citizens feared that the new government could take away certain rights, just as the British had done when they were colonies. They decided to add ten amendments to the Constitution—the Bill of Rights—guaranteeing freedom of religion, speech, assembly, and other protections we take for granted today. This book vividly describes how the Bill of Rights came into existence. It will be enjoyed by students and valued by teachers.
Paperback, 978-0-7641-4021-1, $6.99, *Can$8.50*

To order—Available at your local book store or visit **www.barronseduc.com**

Barron's Educational Series, Inc.
250 Wireless Blvd.
Hauppauge, N.Y. 11788
Order toll-free: 1-800-645-3476
Order by fax: 1-631-434-3217

In Canada:
Georgetown Book Warehouse
34 Armstrong Ave.
Georgetown, Ontario L7G 4R9
Canadian orders: 1-800-247-7160
Order by fax: 1-800-887-1594

Prices subject to
change without notice.

(#133) R3/16